A Disciple's Journal
Year C

Advent 2021, 2024, 2027, 2030

A Guide for Daily Prayer,
Bible Reading, and Discipleship

Steven W. Manskar
with Melanie C. Gordon
& Taylor Burton-Edwards

DISCIPLESHIP
RESOURCES
NASHVILLE

ISBN: 978-0-88177-954-7

At the time of publication all websites referenced in this book were valid. However, due to the fluid nature of the internet, some addresses may have changed or the content may no longer be relevant.

Upper Room Books® website: upperroombooks.com

Cover design: Bruce Gore, GoreStudio, Inc.
Cover image: Unsplash.com
Typsetting and interior design: PerfecType, Nashville, TN

DR954

"O that we may all receive of Christ's fullness,
grace upon grace;
grace to pardon our sins, and subdue our iniquities;
to justify our persons and to sanctify our souls;
and to complete that holy change, that renewal of our hearts,
whereby we may be transformed
into that blessed image wherein thou didst create us."

→ John Wesley ←

Contents

Lent

Holy Week

Easter

The Season After Pentecost (Ordinary Time)

Wesleyan Discipleship

O that we could begin this day
in devout meditations,
in joy unspeakable,
and in blessing and praising thee,
who hast given us such good hope
and everlasting consolation.
Lift up our minds
above all these little things below,
which are apt to distract our thoughts;
and keep them above,
till our hearts are fully bent
to seek thee every day,
in the way wherein
Jesus hath gone before us,
though it should be with
the loss of all we here possess.

JOHN WESLEY
A Collection of Prayers for Families

How to Use *A Disciple's Journal*

John Wesley encouraged Christians to pray and read scripture at the beginning and the end of every day. *A Disciple's Journal* is designed to help you habitually open your heart to grace by beginning and ending each day in the presence of the Triune God.

A Disciple's Journal contains two facing pages for each week of the year:

- **The left-hand page** is a guide for daily Bible reading with the Revised Common Lectionary Daily Readings.

  Sunday, the Lord's Day, is at the center. The lessons for Thursday, Friday, and Saturday are selected to prepare you for Sunday. The lessons for Monday, Tuesday, and Wednesday are selected to help you reflect upon Sunday.

  Lessons from the Old and New Testament are selected for each day of the week. The New Testament lessons for Saturday and Wednesday are from one of the Gospels.

  The lectionary includes two periods outside the seasons of Lent, Easter, Advent, and Christmas called Ordinary Time. The thirty-three or thirty-four Sundays that fall in the periods after the Baptism of the Lord and after Pentecost form a distinct sequence and are guided by the Gospel of the year.

  The Sundays of Ordinary Time after Epiphany are designated by the number of weeks after Epiphany, January 6. The length of this first Ordinary Time is determined by Ash Wednesday. Use the daily lectionary for Transfiguration Sunday for the week that includes Ash Wednesday.

  The Sundays of Ordinary Time after Pentecost are designated "Sunday between [Month] [Date] and [Date] inclusive." For example: "Sunday between May 24 and 28 inclusive."

  The bottom half of the page is divided into four quadrants that correspond to the General Rule of Discipleship (see pages 178-179). Use this space to record your acts of compassion, justice, worship, and devotion during the week.

- **The right-hand page** contains portions of hymns by Charles Wesley and excerpts from sermons by John Wesley, unless otherwise indicated. You will also find a prayer for each week based upon the Sunday scripture lessons. These prayers are written by members of the Consultation on Common Texts (www.commontexts.org). They are used here by permission.

If you are in a Covenant Discipleship group (see pages 182-184) or another type of small group, bring *A Disciple's Journal* to your weekly meeting. It will help you remember what you have done during the week. You may also record prayer concerns from the group.

The Daily Lectionary

A lectionary is a systematic way of reading the Bible guided by the church's liturgical calendar. It unites the global church in prayer and worship. The daily lectionary used in *A Disciple's Journal* was developed by the Consultation on Common Texts (commontexts.org). It is used here by permission.

The Revised Common Lectionary (RCL) is organized as a three-year cycle. Each year emphasizes one of the Synoptic Gospels. Year C is shaped by the Gospel According to Luke, with significant portions of the Gospel According to John included during Lent and Easter. Because the RCL is intended for use in Sunday worship, it necessarily neglects significant portions of the Bible. The daily lectionary fills in the gaps.

Four scripture lessons are selected for Sunday; two lessons from the Old Testament and two lessons from the New Testament. The first text is from the historical, wisdom, or prophetic books. The second is a psalm that reflects a theme from the first lesson. The third lesson is from one of the epistles. And the final lesson is from one of the Gospels.

Prayer in the Morning and at Night

Pages 20 through 23 contain guides for daily prayer in the morning and at night. They are adapted from *The Book of Common Prayer*, which was the prayer book of John and Charles Wesley.

The collects for each day of the week are ancient prayers of the church. Praying these simple guides of daily prayer with the collects is a way of joining your prayers with Christians around the world and throughout history.

The Psalm

Two psalms are appointed for most weeks. The first psalm is read with the lessons selected for Thursday, Friday, and Saturday. This psalm is also read, chanted, or sung in Sunday worship. The second psalm is read with the lessons assigned for Monday, Tuesday, and Wednesday.

Read the psalm to prepare your heart and mind before you read the other texts for the day. Reading the same psalm for several days helps you dwell in God's Word. Listen for what God is saying to you, the church, and the world. Conclude the psalm by saying or singing the Gloria Patri:

> **Glory to the Father, and to the Son, and to the Holy Spirit:**
> **as it was in the beginning, is now, and will be forever. Amen.**

The Hymn

A Charles Wesley hymn is provided each week. Hymns are an important resource for Christian formation in the Wesleyan tradition. Like the psalms, the hymn for the week may be either said or sung each day. Take time to reflect upon the words and allow them to open your heart to God and God's grace. Let them become part of you. Memorize the hymn along with the psalms.

A Cycle of Intercession

To help broaden your daily prayer, "A Cycle of Intercession" is provided beginning on page 25. In the Lord's Prayer, Jesus instructs us to pray, "Your kingdom come, your will be done, on earth as in heaven." The cycle of intercession encourages us to pray for the world each day.

A Blessing

I pray that *A Disciple's Journal* will be a blessing to you and your small group. If you are not in a small group for mutual accountability and support for growth in holiness of heart and life, I pray that you will find or form one.

> "Let us hold fast to the confession of our hope without wavering, for he who has promised is faithful. And let us consider how to provoke one another to love and good deeds, not neglecting to meet together, as is the habit of some, but encouraging one another, and all the more as you see the Day approaching." (Hebrews 10:23-35)

Rev. Steven W. Manskar, D. Min.
Grand Rapids, Michigan
steven.manskar@gmail.com

Using *A Disciple's Journal* with Your Small Group

A Disciple's Journal is an excellent small-group resource. The following are some examples of how the *Journal* may be used to help form disciples of Jesus Christ in small groups:

- Adopt the General Rule of Discipleship as your group's rule of life. Use the *Journal* to record how you have witnessed to Jesus Christ in the world and followed his teachings through acts of compassion, justice, worship, and devotion under the guidance of the Holy Spirit.
  - » The General Rule provides the agenda when the group meets.
  - » Begin with a prayer; read one of the scripture lessons for the day; ask, "What is God saying to us in this lesson today?"
  - » The leader then asks people in turn, beginning with himself or herself, "How is it with your soul?" The General Rule of Discipleship guides people as they respond to the question.
  - » The group prays for each person after they've shared their response.
  - » The meeting concludes with singing a hymn, sharing prayer concerns, and praying the prayer for the week from *A Disciple's Journal.*
  - » Each quarter, identify a specific area of the General Rule of Discipleship on which each person (or the group as a whole) wants to focus and grow; review the group's prayer concerns and goals.
- Advent, Lenten, and Easter study groups read the scripture lessons for each day of the season and discuss the various themes, ideas, and images that emerge when they meet. Pray the prayer for each week along with the recommendations in the Cycle of Intercession.
- Groups may read and discuss the excerpts from John Wesley's sermon provided for that week.
- Read, reflect, and discuss the hymns of Charles Wesley. His poetry is a rich resource for study, theological reflection, and prayer.

Using *A Disciple's Journal* as a Family

Melanie C. Gordon

Ye that are truly kind parents, in the morning, in the evening, and all the day beside, press upon all your children, "to walk in love, as Christ also loved us, and gave himself for us;" to mind that one point, "God is love; and he that dwelleth in love, dwelleth in God, and God in him."
—John Wesley, *On the Education of Children*

John Wesley was committed to the education and formation of children. In his sermons *On the Education of Children* and *On Family Religion,* Wesley emphasizes children's holiness and fitness for eternal joy with God and the important role of parents in helping their children "walk in love." Praying together as a family is a tradition in Christian households. When we pray as a family, we connect with one another in a way that deepens intimacy with one another and with God. Whether we gather around the kitchen table, in the family room, or via technology when our families cannot be physically present with one another, daily prayer as a family offers the opportunity to grow in faith as children of God. The Gospels are clear that we are to make the way clear for children to discover Jesus. This is imperative in the church community and in our homes, where parents are the first and most-significant teachers of their children. The home should be considered a sacred shelter, a place where "unconditional love, affirmation, challenges to accountability, and forgiveness are known; to learn and share rituals, symbols, and stories of faith; to recognize and claim their special gifts and mission in the world" (*Family the Forming Center*, Marjorie Thompson, p. 144).

As the world pulls parents in many directions, finding intentional time with our families can be challenging. Scripture tells us to teach children the words of God: "Recite them to your children. Talk about them when you are sitting around your house and when you are out and about, when you are lying down and when you are getting up" (Deuteronomy 6:7 CEB). Taking time to engage with one another and the world daily, strengthened by the love of God, is most effective when done in a pattern of time and rhythm. Family rituals create a sense of belonging, allowing each member to understand what is important in the family and offering a sense of identity. Rituals provide rhythm and consistency to our lives, allowing us to move spiritually from one place to another. Through ritual comes healing, connection, and growth. What is realistic for a family that needs to get children up, dressed, fed, and off to school? What is realistic for families whose children are involved in activities after school, then homework, followed by dinner and bedtime? Each family has its own rhythm, and this guide is designed for families to create a rhythm in their life that intentionally includes time for family prayer, scripture, and discipleship. Look at this as not just one more thing to put on an already hectic schedule. See this as a way to grow closer to God as a family, thereby helping children to engage in the world equipped as representatives of God in the world.

Setting the Space

Create a holy space or sacred space within the home. This can be as simple as a corner in the family room that contains symbols of faith—a candle, a cross, a small container of water, a cup, prayer beads, and a children's Bible. Take some time to ask your children what they think of when they think of God's love, and search the house for symbols that represent this.

Prayer boxes provide a concrete and safe place for children to share their prayers with God. Not all of us are comfortable praying aloud, and some children do not possess the language to share what is on their hearts. Writing or drawing their prayers offers children a way to release what they are feeling, and hold on to these feelings while sharing them with God.

Prayer beads provide a tangible way for children to relate to God. There are several ways to use prayer beads. Each bead can represent a prayer for a specific person or situation; beads can be held in the hand as a reminder of our connection with God, or beads can be used as the Israelites held fringe in their hands to remember that God will never abandon them.

Candles are a way to remind children that God is with us. Light a candle as you begin your daily prayers as a symbol that Christ is the light of the world. Encourage children to carefully blow out the candle at the end of your family prayers to symbolize taking the light out into the world as representatives of Christ in the world.

During Daily Prayers

Sharing scripture with children of different ages can be a challenge, and the assigned daily Bible reading may be a bit overwhelming for children to sit through each day. Read the scripture ahead of time. Use a Bible translation that children will connect with. After you read the scripture, simply share the narrative with your children in a way you know they will understand.

Bless your children each day, as each is a blessing from God who needs to hear that on a regular basis. After daily prayers, take a moment and get on the physical level of each child; look each child in the eye; and with your thumb or pointing finger, make the sign of the cross on their forehead and say, "You are a blessing." Children love being reminded that they are blessings in our lives.

Extending Daily Prayers

Three ways to use the Jerusalem cross as a visual reminder for children:

- **Make a copy** of the Jerusalem cross to place on the refrigerator or a central place in your home as a reminder for children of how we love God and offer God's love to others.
- **Let children draw a copy** of the Jerusalem cross, and then encourage them to draw or write how they have lived into works of piety and mercy each week.
- Since we live in a culture where we are often on the go, **keep a copy** of the Jerusalem cross in the car as a conversation starter for children to share how they have experienced acts of worship, justice, devotion, and compassion.

Taking the Light of God into the World

Serve the community as a family. Balancing our works of piety with works of mercy will allow us, and our children, to live into the command to love God and neighbor. Use the Jerusalem cross as a guide to help children find ways in which you can serve others through acts of compassion and justice.

Children notice the world around them with awe and wonder, offering adults the opportunity to appreciate the world through their eyes if we will only take the time. Use time in the car, on the bus, or on the train to ask them what they noticed today that reminded them of something from morning prayer. They may need a little prompting, so ask them what they noticed during the day. You may also want to ask them what they wondered about today.

A Guide for Prayer as a Family

PRAYER IN THE MORNING

Call to Prayer

The Call to Prayer in A Disciple's Journal *is quite appropriate for family daily prayer.*

Scripture

Choose one text to share from an age-appropriate translation of the Bible.

Silence

Keep the time for silent reflection appropriate for the ages of your children. As you practice as a family, the silence will become more focused and comfortable for the children.

Hymn

There are a couple of options for hymn singing. Recite or sing the hymn together, and ask the children which words stood out for them. You may also want to choose a hymn that they enjoy singing and make it a regular morning hymn.

Prayers for Ourselves and Others

Offer children the space to share their prayers. You may want to teach them the response, "Lord, hear our prayer" *following each prayer.*

The Lord's Prayer

The Collect

Use the list of Collects for Families appointed for each day. If your children are readers and feel comfortable, allow them to take turns reading the Collects.

Blessing

Make the sign of the cross on each child's forehead and say, "As you go through your day, remember that you are a blessing" *or* "You are a blessing" *or* "Remember that you are a blessing."

Collects for Morning Prayer

SUNDAY

Almighty God, you are the source of all that is glorious. Fill our hearts with your gladness today, and in all we do today, help us worship you with gladness, through Jesus Christ and in the Holy Spirit. Amen.

MONDAY

All-knowing God, you offer great guidance for us each day. Open our hearts and minds that we will follow you joyfully through the challenges of the day, through Jesus Christ and in the Holy Spirit. Amen.

TUESDAY

God of peace, you sent Jesus as the Prince of Peace. Open our hearts that we will offer peace to people we encounter today, through Jesus Christ and in the Holy Spirit. Amen.

WEDNESDAY

God of grace, you offer us grace that we do not always deserve. As we encounter people today, help us to remember and extend grace to them, through Jesus Christ and in the Holy Spirit. Amen.

THURSDAY

Most Holy God, you are the greatest guide we will ever have in our lives. As we go about our day today, help us to remember that you will guide us through any challenges, through Jesus Christ and in the Holy Spirit. Amen.

FRIDAY

Most Holy God, you created a world filled with mystery and wonder. In all we do today, help us to notice the beauty of this world, through Jesus Christ and in the Holy Spirit. Amen.

SATURDAY

Lord God, you gave us a world to care for and serve. As we go through this day, help us to notice and respond to ways we can serve you, through Jesus Christ and in the Holy Spirit. Amen.

PRAYER AT NIGHT

Call to Prayer

The Call to Prayer for Night Prayer in A Disciple's Journal *(see page 22) is quite appropriate for family daily prayer.*

Scripture

Reread the scripture text that you and your family shared during morning prayer. Offer children an opportunity to share what they notice about the scripture reading.

Prayers for Ourselves and Others

Offer children the space to share their prayers. You may want to teach them the response, "Lord, hear our prayer" *following each prayer.*

The Lord's Prayer

The Collect

Use the same Collect for Evening each night to conclude the day with something that is familiar and offers security.

Blessing

Make the sign of the cross on each child's forehead and say, "As you go to sleep tonight, remember that you are a blessing" *or* "You are a blessing" *or* "Remember that you are a blessing."

Collect for Evening

Lord, Jesus Christ, you made this day,
    and you surrounded our work and play with your love all day.
Thank you for watching over us
    and bringing us together tonight as a family of God.
Bless and watch over us through the night. Amen.

Find a list of Bibles and books for children at http://bit.ly/2o0gEjG.

Family Prayer While Traveling

Our work and responsibilities outside of the home can take us away from our families for periods of time. **When you cannot be with your children**, adapt the daily prayers and Bible reading to share over the telephone or video technology to keep you connected to one another and God. To stay connected, let your children choose a symbol of faith that you can take with you on your trip. Plan a time for each morning and evening to connect. Use the Jerusalem cross to share ways in which each person offered compassion or addressed a social issue. This will open conversation about joys and sorrows of the day. Continue with a prayer, followed by the Lord's Prayer, the Collect for Families, and a blessing for your children.

When you travel as a family, let the children choose a symbol or symbols to carry with them. Plan a time for the family to connect each morning and evening that you are away. Ideally, continue the same family ritual of daily prayers. If this is not possible, choose a space to gather as a family. Use the Jerusalem cross to share ways in which each person offered compassion or addressed a social issue. Begin with a prayer, followed by the Lord's Prayer, the Collect for Families, and a blessing for your children. This will continue the consistency and rhythm that children need to feel loved and secure.

Prayer in the Morning and at Night

A Cycle of Intercession

Morning Prayer

CALL TO PRAYER (from Psalm 51)
> Open my lips, O Lord,
>> and my mouth shall proclaim your praise.
>
> Create in me a clean heart, O God,
>> and renew a right spirit within me.
>
> Glory to the Father, and to the Son, and to the Holy Spirit:
>> as it was in the beginning, is now, and will be forever. Amen.

SCRIPTURE *The psalm and one or both of the lessons for the day are read.*

SILENCE *What captured your imagination?*
What is God up to in this text for your mission today?

HYMN *The hymn for the week may be said or sung;*
the Apostles' Creed (see page 24) may be said.

PRAYERS FOR OURSELVES AND FOR OTHERS
> *See* A Cycle of Intercession *on pages 25–27.*

THE LORD'S PRAYER
> Our Father in heaven, hallowed be your Name,
>> your kingdom come,
>> your will be done, on earth as in heaven.
>
> Give us today our daily bread.
> Forgive us our sins
>> as we forgive those who sin against us.
>
> Save us from the time of trial,
>> and deliver us from evil.
>
> For the kingdom, the power,
>> and the glory are yours,
>> now and for ever. Amen.

THE PRAYERS *The collect for the day of the week (see page 21) and/or the*
prayer for the week is said.

Collects for the Morning

SUNDAY

O God, you make us glad with the weekly remembrance of the glorious resurrection of your Son our Lord: Give us this day such blessing through our worship of you, that the week to come may be spent in your favor; through Jesus Christ our Lord. Amen.

MONDAY (*for Renewal of Life*)

O God, the King eternal, whose light divides the day from the night and turns the shadow of death into the morning: Drive far from us all wrong desires, incline our hearts to keep your law, and guide our feet into the way of peace; that, having done your will with cheerfulness during the day, we may, when night comes, rejoice to give you thanks; through Jesus Christ our Lord. Amen.

TUESDAY (*for Peace*)

O God, the author of peace and lover of concord, to know you is eternal life and to serve you is perfect freedom: Defend us, your humble servants, in all assaults of our enemies; that we, surely trusting in your defense, may not fear the power of any adversaries; through the might of Jesus Christ our Lord. Amen.

WEDNESDAY (*for Grace*)

Lord God, almighty and everlasting Father, you have brought us in safety to this new day: Preserve us with your mighty power, that we may not fall into sin, nor be overcome by adversity; and in all we do, direct us to the fulfilling of your purpose; through Jesus Christ our Lord. Amen.

THURSDAY (*for Guidance*)

Heavenly Father, in you we live and move and have our being: We humbly pray you so to guide and govern us by your Holy Spirit, that in all the cares and occupations of our life we may not forget you, but may remember that we are ever walking in your sight; through Jesus Christ our Lord. Amen.

FRIDAY

Almighty God, whose most dear Son went not up to joy but first he suffered pain, and entered not into glory before he was crucified: Mercifully grant that we, walking in the way of the cross, may find it none other than the way of life and peace; through Jesus Christ your Son our Lord. Amen.

SATURDAY

Almighty God, who after the creation of the world rested from all your works and sanctified a day of rest for all your creatures: Grant that we, putting away all earthly anxieties, may be duly prepared for the service of your sanctuary, and that our rest here upon earth may be a preparation for the eternal rest promised to your people in heaven; through Jesus Christ our Lord. Amen.

Night Prayer

CALL TO PRAYER

O gracious Light,
    pure brightness of the everliving Father in heaven,
O Jesus Christ, holy and blessed!
Now as we come to the setting of the sun,
    and our eyes behold the evening light,
        we sing your praises, O God: Father, Son, and Holy Spirit.
You are worthy at all times to be praised by happy voices,
    O Son of God, O Giver of life,
and to be glorified through all the worlds.

SCRIPTURE   *The psalm and one or both of the lessons for the day may be read.*

PRAYERS FOR OURSELVES AND FOR OTHERS

Recall and examine your day. When did you meet Christ?
When did you deny Christ? When did you serve Christ?

THE LORD'S PRAYER

Our Father in heaven, hallowed be your Name,
    your kingdom come,
    your will be done, on earth as in heaven.
Give us today our daily bread.
Forgive us our sins
    as we forgive those who sin against us.
Save us from the time of trial,
    and deliver us from evil.
For the kingdom, the power,
    and the glory are yours,
    now and for ever. Amen.

THE COLLECT   *The collect for the day of the week (see page 23) and/or the*
                prayer for the week are said.

Collects for the Night

SUNDAY

Lord God, whose Son our Savior Jesus Christ triumphed over the powers of death and prepared for us our place in the new Jerusalem: Grant that we, who have this day given thanks for his resurrection, may praise you in that City of which he is the light, and where he lives and reigns for ever and ever. Amen.

MONDAY

Most holy God, the source of all good desires, all right judgments, and all just works: Give to us, your servants, that peace which the world cannot give, so that our minds may be fixed on the doing of your will, and that we, being delivered from the fear of all enemies, may live in peace and quietness; through the mercies of Christ Jesus our Savior. Amen.

TUESDAY

Be our light in the darkness, O Lord, and in your great mercy defend us from all perils and dangers of this night; for the love of your only Son, our Savior Jesus Christ. Amen.

WEDNESDAY

O God, the life of all who live, the light of the faithful, the strength of those who labor, and the repose of the dead: We thank you for the blessings of the day that is past, and humbly ask for your protection through the coming night. Bring us in safety to the morning hours; through him who died and rose again for us, your Son our Savior Jesus Christ. Amen.

THURSDAY

Lord Jesus, stay with us, for evening is at hand and the day is past; be our companion in the way, kindle our hearts, and awaken hope, that we may know you as you are revealed in scripture and the breaking of bread. Grant this for the sake of your love. Amen.

FRIDAY

Lord Jesus Christ, by your death you took away the sting of death: Grant to us your servants so to follow in faith where you have led the way, that we may at length fall asleep peacefully in you and wake up in your likeness; for your tender mercies' sake. Amen.

SATURDAY

O God, the source of eternal light: Shed forth your unending day upon us who watch for you, that our lips may praise you, our lives may bless you, and our worship tomorrow give you glory; through Jesus Christ our Lord. Amen.

The Apostles' Creed

I believe in God, the Father almighty,
    creator of heaven and earth.
I believe in Jesus Christ, his only Son our Lord,
    who was conceived by the Holy Spirit,
    and born of the Virgin Mary,
    suffered under Pontius Pilate,
        was crucified, died, and was buried;
        he descended to the dead.
    On the third day he rose again;
    he ascended into heaven,
        is seated at the right hand of the Father,
        and will come again to judge the living and the dead.
I believe in the Holy Spirit,
    the holy catholic church,
    the communion of saints,
    the forgiveness of sins,
    the resurrection of the body,
    and the life everlasting. Amen.

Wesley Covenant Prayer

I am no longer my own, but thine.
Put me to what thou wilt, rank me with whom thou wilt.
Put me to doing, put me to suffering.
Let me be employed by thee or laid aside for thee,
    exalted for thee or brought low for thee.
Let me be full, let me be empty.
Let me have all things, let me have nothing.
I freely and heartily yield all things
    to thy pleasure and disposal.
And now, O glorious and blessed God,
    Father, Son, and Holy Spirit,
    thou art mine, and I am thine. So be it.
And the covenant which I have made on earth,
    let it be ratified in heaven. Amen.

A Cycle of Intercession

Prayers may include the following concerns if it is desired to pray for different topics through the week and the seasons.

Every day
- In the morning: the day and its tasks; the world and its needs; the church and its life
- In the evening: peace; individuals and their needs

In Ordinary Time

Sunday

- The universal church
- Bishops, annual conferences, central conferences, and all who lead the church
- The leaders of the nations
- The natural world and the resources of the earth
- All who are in any kind of need

Monday

- The media and the arts
- Farming and fishing
- Commerce and industry
- Those whose work is unfulfilling, stressful, or fraught with danger
- All who are unemployed

Tuesday

- All who are sick in body, mind, or spirit
- Those in the midst of famine or disaster
- Victims of abuse and violence, intolerance and prejudice
- Those who are bereaved
- All who work in the medical and healing professions

Wednesday

- The social services
- All who work in the criminal justice system
- Victims and perpetrators of crime
- The work of aid agencies throughout the world
- Those living in poverty or under oppression

Thursday

- Local government and community leaders
- All who provide local services
- Those who work with young or elderly people
- Schools, colleges, and universities
- Emergency and rescue organizations

Friday

- The president of the United States, members of Congress, and the armed forces
- Peace and justice in the world
- Those who work for reconciliation
- All whose lives are devastated by war and civil strife
- Prisoners, refugees, and homeless people

Saturday

- Our homes, families, friends, and all whom we love
- Those whose time is spent caring for others
- Those who are close to death
- Those who have lost hope
- The worship of the church

In Seasonal Time

Advent

- The church, that it may be ready for the coming of Christ
- The leaders of the church
- The nations, that they may be subject to the rule of God
- Those who are working for justice in the world
- The broken, that they may find God's healing

Christmas

- The church, especially in places of conflict
- The Holy Land, for peace with justice and reconciliation
- Refugees and asylum seekers
- Homeless people
- Families with young children

Epiphany
- The unity of the church
- The peace of the world
- The revelation of Christ to those from whom his glory is hidden
- All who travel

Lent
- Those preparing for baptism and confirmation
- Those serving through leadership
- Those looking for forgiveness
- Those misled by the false gods of this present age
- All who are hungry

Holy Week
- The persecuted church
- The oppressed peoples of the world
- All who are lonely
- All who are near to death
- All who are facing loss

Easter
- The people of God, that they may proclaim the risen Lord
- God's creation, that the peoples of the earth may meet their responsibility to care
- Those in despair and darkness, that they may find the hope and light of Christ
- Those in fear of death, that they may find faith through the Resurrection
- Prisoners and captives

Ascension until Pentecost
- Those who wait on God, that they may find renewal
- The earth, for productivity and for fruitful harvests
- All who are struggling with broken relationships

All Saints until Advent
- The saints on earth, that they may live as citizens of heaven
- All people, that they may hear and believe the word of God
- All who fear the winter months
- All political leaders, that they may imitate the righteous rule of Christ
- All who grieve or wait with the dying

O that we might heartily surrender our wills to thine;
that we may unchangeably cleave unto it,
with the greatest and most entire affection to all thy commands.
O that there may abide for ever in us
such a strong and powerful sense of thy mighty love
towards us in Christ Jesus,
as may constrain us freely and willingly to please thee,
in the constant exercise of righteousness and mercy,
temperance and charity, meekness and patience,
truth and fidelity;
together with such an humble, contented, and peaceable spirit,
as may adorn the religion of our Lord and Master.
Yea, let it ever be the joy of our hearts to be righteous,
as thou art righteous;
to be merciful, as thou, our heavenly Father, art merciful;
to be holy, as thou who hast called us art holy,
to be endued with thy divine wisdom,
and to resemble thee in faithfulness and truth.
O that the example of our blessed Savior
may be always dear unto us,
that we may cheerfully follow him in every holy temper,
and delight to do thy will, O God.
Let these desires, which thou hast given us,
never die or languish in our hearts,
but be kept always alive, always in their vigor and force,
by the perpetual inspirations of the Holy Ghost.

JOHN WESLEY
A Collection of Prayers for Families

A Disciple's Journal
Year C

Help us to build each other up,
Our little stock improve;
Increase our faith, confirm our hope,
And perfect us in love.

CHARLES WESLEY

The Christian Year

The Christian Year organizes the worship of the church to help Christians rehearse the life and ministry of Jesus and to disciple others in his way. The Christian Year combines evangelism, teaching, worship, the formation of disciples, and mission, and helps the church keep all of these vital elements of its life and ministry constantly before it.

Advent

Orientation to Ultimate Salvation

The Christian Year begins with the end in mind. Advent is the season for orienting Christians to our place within God's work of salvation of the cosmos. Advent focuses primarily on the fulfillment of all things in Jesus Christ. It begins by reminding us of the second advent (coming) of Christ, the final judgment, the resurrection of the dead, and new creation. We then spend two weeks with the prophet known as John the Baptizer, whose ministry and preaching about the judgment and end of this current age laid the groundwork for the teaching and ministry of Jesus. The final Sunday of Advent brings us to events leading up to the birth of Jesus.

Advent starts to work in us like a funnel. The purpose of a funnel is to concentrate everything that can flow into it into a smaller outlet so everything can fit into a smaller space. Advent takes in all of history from the "top" and concentrates it and all its meanings on one person, Jesus Christ. It takes in all time, past and future, and moving backward in time, leads us to the incarnation of God in Jesus Christ. It takes in the whole cosmos and its complete renewal and leads us to the confusing and messy—which is to say, very human—circumstances surrounding the birth of Jesus. It challenges us to take in the infinitely vast and incomprehensible and to see, hear, and feel how all of it flows out of the son of Mary.

But the aim of Advent is not to fill up our heads with grand ideas. Advent, like the age to come it proclaims again and again, is intended to do nothing less than call us to repent and live the good news that God's kingdom, which will complete all that Advent describes, has drawn near.

This is why Advent was initially designed as a secondary season for preparing persons for baptism. Just as those preparing for baptism during Lent would be baptized at Easter, so those preparing for baptism during Advent would be baptized during Christmas Season, primarily on Epiphany.

As you read and pray daily this Advent, allow the funnel to do its orienting and reorienting work in you. But more than this, expect the Spirit's refilling, even now, to make all things new in you.

Rev. Taylor Burton-Edwards

First Sunday of Advent

Preparation for Sunday
Daily: Psalm 25:1-10

Thursday
Nehemiah 9:6-15
1 Thessalonians 5:1-11

Friday
Nehemiah 9:16-25
1 Thessalonians 5:12-22

Saturday
Nehemiah 9:26-31
Luke 21:20-24

Sunday
Jeremiah 33:14-16
Psalm 25:1-10
1 Thessalonians 3:9-13
Luke 21:25-36

Reflection on Sunday
Daily: Psalm 90

Monday
Numbers 17:1-11
2 Peter 3:1-18

Tuesday
2 Samuel 7:18-29
Revelation 22:12-16

Wednesday
Isaiah 1:24-31
Luke 11:29-32

The General Rule of Discipleship
To witness to Jesus Christ in the world and to follow his teachings
through acts of compassion, justice, worship, and devotion under the guidance of the Holy Spirit.

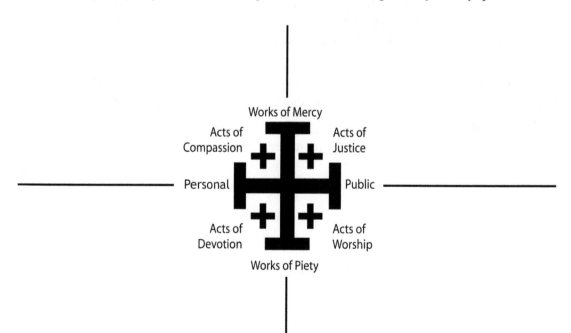

A Word from John Wesley

All the blessings which God hath bestowed upon man are of his mere grace, bounty, or favour: his free, undeserved favour; favour altogether undeserved; man having no claim to the least of his mercies. It was free grace that "formed man of the dust of the ground, and breathed into him a living soul," and stamped on that soul the image of God, and "put all things under his feet." The same free grace continues to us, at this day, life, and breath, and all things. For there is nothing we are, or have, or do, which can deserve the least thing at God's hand. "All our works thou, O God, hast wrought in us." These therefore, are so many more instances of free mercy: and whatever righteousness may be found in man, this also is the gift of God.

Sermon 1: "Salvation by Faith," ¶1

A Hymn from Charles Wesley

Hearken to the solemn voice,
The awful midnight cry!
Waiting souls, rejoice, rejoice,
And see the bridegroom nigh!
Lo! he comes to keep his word;
Light and joy his looks impart;
Go ye forth to meet your Lord,
And meet him in your heart.

Wait we all in patient hope
Till Christ the Judge shall come;
We shall soon be all caught up
To meet the general doom;
In an hour to us unknown,
As a thief in deepest night,
Christ shall suddenly come down
With all his saints in light.

Happy he whom Christ shall find
Watching to see him come;
Him the Judge of all mankind
Shall bear triumphant home;
Who can answer to his word?
Which of you dares meet his day?
'Rise, and come to Judgment'—Lord,
We rise, and come away.

(*Collection—1781*, #53:1, 4, & 5)*

Prayers, Comments & Questions

O God of all the prophets, you herald the coming of the Son of man by wondrous signs in the heavens and on the earth. Guard our hearts from despair so that we, in the company of the faithful and by the power of your Holy Spirit, may be found ready to raise our heads at the coming near of our redemption, the day of Jesus Christ. Amen.

*Hymns labeled *Collection—1781* are from *A Collection of Hymns for the use of The People Called Methodists* published by John Wesley in 1781.

Second Sunday of Advent

Preparation for Sunday
Daily: Luke 1:68-79

Thursday
Malachi 3:5-12
Philippians 1:12-18a

Friday
Malachi 3:13-18
Philippians 1:18b-26

Saturday
Malachi 4:1-6
Luke 9:1-6

Sunday
Malachi 3:1-4
Luke 1:68-79
Philippians 1:3-11
Luke 3:1-6

Reflection on Sunday
Daily: Psalm 126

Monday
Isaiah 40:1-11
Romans 8:22-25

Tuesday
Isaiah 19:18-25
2 Peter 1:2-15

Wednesday
Isaiah 35:3-7
Luke 7:18-30

The General Rule of Discipleship
To witness to Jesus Christ in the world and to follow his teachings
through acts of compassion, justice, worship, and devotion under the guidance of the Holy Spirit.

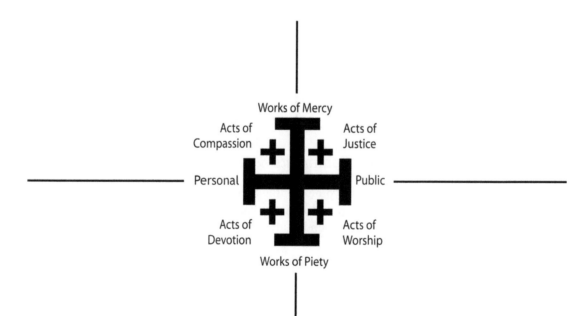

A Word from John Wesley

If it be inquired, "What more than this is implied in the being 'altogether a Christian?'" I answer: First, the love of God. For thus saith his Word: "Thou shalt love the Lord thy God with all thy heart, and with all thy soul, and with all thy mind, and with all thy strength." Such a love is this, as engrosses the whole heart, as takes up all the affections, as fills the entire capacity of the soul and employs the utmost extent of all its faculties. He that thus loves the Lord his God, his spirit continually "rejoiceth in God his Saviour."

Sermon 2: "The Almost Christian," § II.1

A Hymn from Charles Wesley

He comes! he comes! the Judge severe!
The seventh trumpet speaks him near;
His light'nings flash, his thunders roll;
How welcome to the faithful soul!

From heaven angelic voices sound,
See the almighty Jesus crowned!
Girt with omnipotence and grace,
And glory decks the Saviour's face!

Descending on his azure throne,
He claims the kingdoms for his own;
The kingdoms all obey his word,
And hail him their triumphant Lord!

Shout all the people of the sky,
And all the saints of the Most High;
Our Lord, who now his right obtains,
For ever and for ever reigns.

(*Collection—1781, #55*)

Prayers, Comments & Questions

Out of the embrace of mercy and righteousness, you have brought forth joy and dignity for your people, O Holy One of Israel. Remember now your ancient promise: Make straight the paths that lead to you, and smooth the rough ways, that in our day we might bring forth your compassion for all humanity. Amen.

Third Sunday of Advent

Preparation for Sunday
Daily: Isaiah 12:2-6

Thursday
Amos 6:1-8
2 Corinthians 8:1-15

Friday
Amos 8:4-12
2 Corinthians 9:1-15

Saturday
Amos 9:8-15
Luke 1:57-66

Sunday
Zephaniah 3:14-20
Isaiah 12:2-6
Philippians 4:4-7
Luke 3:7-18

Reflection on Sunday
Daily: Isaiah 11:1-9

Monday
Numbers 16:1-19
Hebrews 13:7-17

Tuesday
Numbers 16:20-35
Acts 28:23-31

Wednesday
Micah 4:8-13
Luke 7:31-35

The General Rule of Discipleship
To witness to Jesus Christ in the world and to follow his teachings
through acts of compassion, justice, worship, and devotion under the guidance of the Holy Spirit.

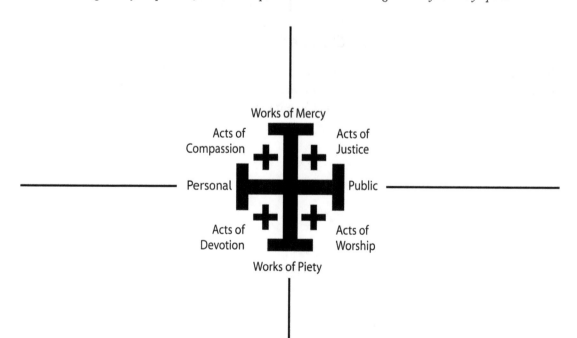

A Word from John Wesley

God is light, and will give himself to every awakened sinner that waiteth for him; and thou shalt then be a temple of the living God, and Christ shall "dwell in thy heart by faith." And, "being rooted and grounded in love," thou shalt be able to comprehend with all saints what is the breadth, and length, and depth, and height of that "love of Christ which passeth knowledge."

Sermon 3: "Awake, Thou That Sleepest," §III.2

A Hymn from Charles Wesley

Ye virgin souls arise,
With all the dead awake.
Unto salvation wise,
Oil in your vessels take:
Upstarting at the midnight cry,
Behold the heavenly bridegroom nigh.

He comes, he comes to call
The nations to his bar,
And raise to glory all
Who fit for glory are;
Made ready for your full reward,
Go forth with joy to meet your Lord.

Then let us wait to hear
The trumpet's welcome sound,
To see our Lord appear,
Watching let us be found;
When Jesus doth the heavens bow,
Be found—as, Lord, thou find'st us now!

(*Collection*—1781, #64:1, 2, & 6)

Prayers, Comments & Questions

O God of the exiles and the lost, you promise restoration and wholeness through the power of Jesus Christ. Give us faith to live joyfully, sustained by your promises as we eagerly await the day when they will be fulfilled for all the world to see, through the coming of your Son, Jesus Christ. Amen.

Fourth Sunday of Advent

Preparation for Sunday
Daily: Psalm 80:1-7

Thursday
Jeremiah 31:31-34
Hebrews 10:10-18

Friday
Isaiah 42:10-18
Hebrews 10:32-39

Saturday
Isaiah 66:7-11
Luke 13:31-35

Sunday
Micah 5:2-5a
Luke 1:46b-55 *or*
Psalm 80:1-7
Hebrews 10:5-10
Luke 1:39-55

Reflection on Sunday
Daily: Psalm 113

Monday
Genesis 25:19-28
Colossians 1:15-20

Tuesday
Genesis 30:1-24
Romans 8:18-30

Wednesday
Isaiah 42:14-21
Luke 1:5-25

The General Rule of Discipleship
To witness to Jesus Christ in the world and to follow his teachings
through acts of compassion, justice, worship, and devotion under the guidance of the Holy Spirit.

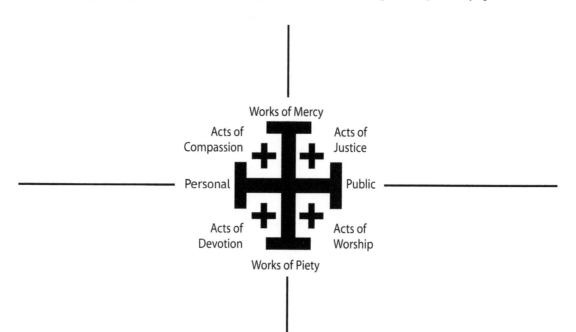

A Word from John Wesley

And, indeed, supposing a few of these lovers of mankind to see "the whole world lying in wickedness," can we believe they would be unconcerned at the sight, at the misery of those for whom their Lord died? Would not their bowels yearn over them, and their hearts melt away for very trouble? Could they then stand idle all the day long even were there no command from him whom they loved? Rather, would they not labour, by all possible means, to pluck some of these brands out of the burning? Undoubtedly they would: they would spare no pains to bring back whomsoever they could of those poor "sheep that had gone astray to the great Shepherd and Bishop of their souls."

Sermon 4: "Scriptural Christianity," § II.2

A Hymn from Charles Wesley

Father our hearts we lift,
Up to thy gracious throne,
And bless thee for the precious gift,
Of thine incarnate Son:
The gift unspeakable,
We thankfully receive,
And to the world thy goodness tell,
And to thy glory live.

Jesus the holy child,
Doth by his birth declare,
That God and man are reconciled,
And one in him we are:
Salvation through his name
To all mankind is given,
And loud his infant cries proclaim,
A peace 'twixt earth and heaven.

(*Hymns for the Nativity of Our Lord*—1745, #9:1 & 2)

Prayers, Comments & Questions

O Shepherd of Israel, you gently support the one who is with child and call forth the Lamb who dances in the womb. Stir our hearts to recognize Christ's coming, as Elizabeth recognized his presence in Mary's radiant obedience to your desire, and open our souls to receive the one who came to love your flock. Amen.

Christmas Season

The Aftermath of Incarnation

After Advent has "funneled" the cosmos into a Palestinian feed bin, Christmas Season opens up for us the global effects of the Word made flesh. Christmas Season is twelve days, starting with the Eve of Christmas, for the church to begin to unpack and wonder anew at all the birth itself began to unleash then and continues to set loose now.

The readings for Christmas Season are full of violence, danger, and, bookended around these stories, blessing. We start and end the season (Christmas Eve and Epiphany) with the joyous announcement of angels to shepherds and magi interpreting the stars. Between them, we encounter the violence of Herod, hear of the genocidal deaths of thousands of male infants, and follow the family of Jesus on a desperate journey into Egypt, not unlike that which the family of Jacob and their offspring had made. We remember the first Christian martyr, the deacon Stephen. We hear of Jesus' circumcision, and we are reminded of the poverty of his family when we learn that the sacrificial animals they could purchase for the rite of purification for Mary were those reserved for the poor.

All of these stories, and others we recount from the Bible, are there to keep us mindful that the kingdoms of this world do not welcome the coming of the kingdom of God but violently resist it. They bear daily witness to the reading from John's Gospel for Christmas Day: "He came to what was his own, and his own people did not accept him" (v. 11). This is why we take the time to prepare people and sponsors for baptism and discipleship. The world as we know it is not set up to receive our witness to Jesus. Indeed, it sets up myriad ways to put our witness to a violent and, from its angle at least, a shameful end.

But in and through all of these stories of opposition, we also remember the earlier words of our reading from Christmas Day: "The light shines in the darkness, and the darkness did not overcome it" (v. 5). And we are called to rehearse through these days, especially if we are accompanying candidates and sponsors toward baptism, that what we are given in Jesus is nothing less than to become, like him, children of God, born not of our own striving but by the will of God through water and the Holy Spirit.

Rev. Taylor Burton-Edwards

Days Around Christmas Day

Daily
Luke 1:46b-55

December 22
Micah 4:1-5
Ephesians 2:11-22

December 23
Micah 4:6-8
2 Peter 1:16-21

December 24
(*Morning*)
Micah 6:6-8
Hebrews 10:5-10

Christmas Day
Isaiah 9:2-7
Psalm 96
Titus 2:11-14
Luke 2:1-20

First Sunday after Christmas Day (Dec. 26–31)
1 Samuel 2:18-20, 26
Psalm 148
Colossians 3:12-17
Luke 2:41-52

Daily
Psalm 148

December 26
2 Chronicles 24:17-24
Acts 6:1-7; 7:51-60

December 27
Proverbs 8:32-36
John 21:19b-24

December 28
Isaiah 54:1-13
Revelation 21:1-7

The General Rule of Discipleship
To witness to Jesus Christ in the world and to follow his teachings
through acts of compassion, justice, worship, and devotion under the guidance of the Holy Spirit.

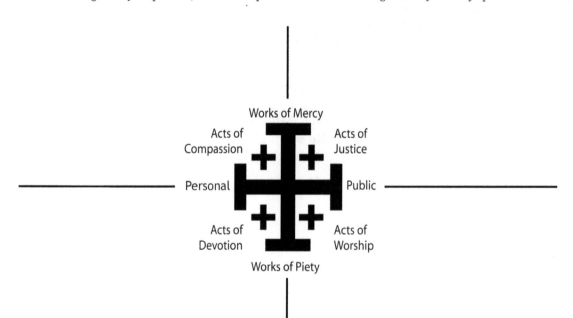

Works of Mercy

Acts of Compassion   Acts of Justice

Personal   Public

Acts of Devotion   Acts of Worship

Works of Piety

A Word from John Wesley

The plain scriptural notion of justification is pardon, the forgiveness of sins. It is that act of God the Father, hereby, for the sake of the propitiation made by the blood of his Son, he "showeth forth his righteousness (or mercy) by the remission of the sins that are past." . . . God will not inflict on that sinner what he deserved to suffer, because the Son of his love hath suffered for him. And from the time we are "accepted through the Beloved," "reconciled to God through his blood," he loves, and blesses, and watches over us for good, even as if we had never sinned.

Sermon 5: "Justification by Faith," § II.5

A Hymn from Charles Wesley

Glory be to God on high,
And peace on earth descend:
God comes down; he bows the sky,
And shews himself our friend!
God, the invisible, appears,
God, the blest, the great I AM,
Sojourns in this vale of tears,
And Jesus is his name.

Him the angels all adored,
Their maker and their King;
Tidings of their humbled Lord,
They now to mortals bring;
Emptied of his majesty,
Of his dazzling glories shorn,
Being's source begins to be,
And God himself is born!

(*Hymns for the Nativity of Our Lord*—1745, #4:1 & 2)

Prayers, Comments & Questions

From our mother's womb you have known us, O God. You call us to follow you through all our days and seek us even when we wander. As we advance in years, clothe us with your love, that we may grow in grace and find favor in your sight; through Jesus Christ. Amen.

Days of Christmas

Daily
Psalm 147:12-20

December 29
1 Chronicles 28:1-10
1 Corinthians 3:10-17

December 30
2 Chronicles 1:7-13
Mark 13:32-37

December 31
1 Kings 3:5-14
John 8:12-19

January 1
Holy Name of Jesus
Numbers 6:22-27
Psalm 8
Galatians 4:4-7 *or*
Philippians 2:5-11
Luke 2:15-21
or
New Year's Day
Ecclesiastes 3:1-13
Psalm 8
Revelation 21:1-6a
Matthew 25:31-46

January 2
Proverbs 1:1-17
James 3:13-18

Second Sunday after
Christmas Day, Jan. 2–5
Jeremiah 31:7-14
Psalm 147:12-20
Ephesians 1:3-14
John 1:1-18

The General Rule of Discipleship
To witness to Jesus Christ in the world and to follow his teachings
through acts of compassion, justice, worship, and devotion under the guidance of the Holy Spirit.

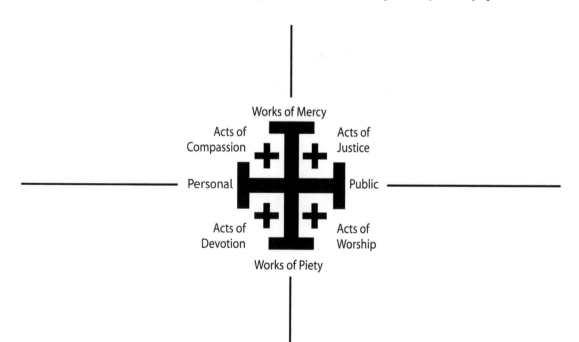

44

A Word from John Wesley

Does then the good Shepherd seek and save only those that are found already? No: He seeks and saves that which is lost. He pardons those who need his pardoning mercy. He saves from the guilt of sin, (and, at the same time, from the power,) sinners of every kind, of every degree: men who, till then, were altogether ungodly; in whom the love of the Father was not; and, consequently, in whom dwelt no good thing, no good or truly Christian temper,—but all such as were evil and abominable,—pride, anger, love of the world,—the genuine fruits of that "carnal mind" which is "enmity against God."

Sermon 5: "Justification by Faith," § III.3

A Hymn from Charles Wesley

See the eternal Son of God,
A mortal son of man,
Dwelling in an earthly clod,
Whom heaven cannot contain!
Stand amazed, ye heavens, at this!
See the Lord of earth and skies!
Humbled to the dust he is,
And in a manger lies!

We the sons of men rejoice,
The Prince of peace proclaim,
With heaven's host lift up our voice,
And shout Immanuel's name:
Knees and hearts to him we bow,
Of our flesh and our bone,
Jesus is our brother now,
And God is all our own!

(*Hymns for the Nativity of Our Lord*—1745, #4:3 & 4)

Prayers, Comments & Questions

Gracious God, you have redeemed us through Jesus Christ, the firstborn of all creation, whose birth we celebrate as the child of Bethlehem. Bless us with every spiritual blessing, that we may live as your adopted children and witness to your glory with unending praise and thanksgiving. Amen.

Days Around Epiphany

Readings through January 9 are provided for use if necessary. When the Epiphany of the Lord is transferred to the preceding Sunday, January 2–5, these dated readings may be used through the week that follows. When the Baptism of the Lord falls on January 11, 12, or 13, the corresponding preparation readings are used after January 9.

Daily
Psalm 72:1-7, 10-14

January 3
Job 42:10-17
Luke 8:16-21

January 4
Isaiah 6:1-5
Acts 7:44-53

January 5
Jeremiah 31:7-14
John 1:1-18

January 6
Epiphany of the Lord
Isaiah 60:1-6
Psalm 72:1-7, 10-14
Ephesians 3:1-12
Matthew 2:1-12

Daily
Psalm 72

January 7
Daniel 2:1-19
Ephesians 4:17—5:1

January 8
Daniel 2:24-49
Ephesians 5:15-20

January 9
Numbers 24:15-19
Luke 1:67-79

The General Rule of Discipleship
To witness to Jesus Christ in the world and to follow his teachings through acts of compassion, justice, worship, and devotion under the guidance of the Holy Spirit.

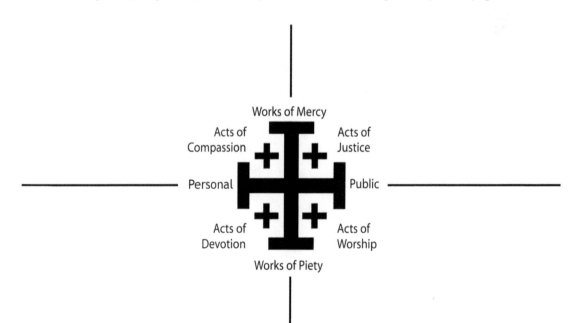

A Word from John Wesley

I am no longer my own, but thine.
Put me to what thou wilt,
    rank me with whom thou wilt. Put me to
doing, put me to suffering. Let me be employed
by thee or
laid aside for thee,
exalted for thee or
brought low for thee.
Let me be full, let me be empty.
Let me have all things,
let me have nothing.
I freely and heartily yield all things
    to thy pleasure and disposal.
And now, O glorious and blessed God, Father,
Son, and Holy Spirit,
    thou art mine, and I am thine.
So be it.
And the covenant
    which I have made on earth,
    let it be ratified in heaven.
Amen.

Wesleyan Covenant Prayer

A Hymn from Charles Wesley

Come, let us use the grace divine,
And all, with one accord,
In a perpetual covenant join
Ourselves to Christ the Lord.

Give up ourselves, through Jesu's power,
His name to glorify;
And promise, in this sacred hour,
For God to live and die.

The covenant we this moment make
Be ever kept in mind:
We will no more our God forsake,
Or cast his words behind.

To each the covenant blood apply,
Which takes our sins away;
And register our names on high,
And keep us to that day.

(*Short Hymns on Select Passages of Holy Scripture*—1762)

Prayers, Comments & Questions

Perfect Light of revelation, as you shone in the life of Jesus, whose epiphany we celebrate, so shine in us and through us, that we may become beacons of truth and compassion, enlightening all creation with deeds of justice and mercy. Amen.

The Season After Epiphany (Ordinary Time)

The Season of Evangelism

The Season after Epiphany is bookended by two celebrations: Baptism of the Lord on the first Sunday after Epiphany and the Transfiguration of Jesus on the last Sunday, prior to Ash Wednesday. The sweep of these Sundays and the days between them prefigures the sweep of the Christian life, from justification and initiation (Baptism of the Lord) to entire sanctification (Transfiguration). While this season is of varying length because of the varying dates of Easter, and so the varying starting time for Ash Wednesday, its purpose is always to help the congregation "get ready to get ready." That is, this is the "introductory course," if you will, to the more intensive preparation for baptism and new commitments in discipleship Lent is designed to help the church undertake.

On the Sundays between Baptism of the Lord and Transfiguration, the Sunday readings from the Old Testament are chosen to correspond with the Gospel readings, which cover the early ministry of Jesus and in particular his calling of disciples. The Old Testament and Gospel readings thus particularly support the evangelistic work of the church reaching out to others during these weeks. The Epistle readings are not chosen to correspond with the other two, but rather to present a "semi-continuous" reading that will be picked up again during the Season after Pentecost. Though the Epistle readings do not directly connect to the gospel, they do still lay out basics of Christian life. One might say that the Epistle readings are there to evangelize the church by helping the church "get its own act together" as it prepares to accompany people in intensive formation in the way of Jesus during Lent.

This gives individuals reading daily and worship leaders planning for weekly celebration two distinct paths they may follow during this season, either of which may contribute to this season's evangelistic purpose. As you undertake your readings through these weeks, you may wish to coordinate the attention you give to the daily readings based on the focus your worship leaders have chosen for Lord's Day worship to gain the maximum benefit from the correlation of the two.

Rev. Taylor Burton-Edwards

First Sunday After the Epiphany: Baptism of the Lord

Preparation for Sunday
Daily: Psalm 29

Thursday
Ecclesiastes 1:1-11
1 Corinthians 1:18-31

Friday
Ecclesiastes 2:1-11
1 Corinthians 2:1-10

Saturday
Ecclesiastes 3:1-15
1 Corinthians 2:11-16

Sunday
Isaiah 43:1-7
Psalm 29
Acts 8:14-17
Luke 3:15-17, 21-22

Reflection on Sunday
Daily: Psalm 106:1-12

Monday
Judges 4:1-16
Ephesians 6:10-17

Tuesday
Judges 5:12-21
1 John 5:13-21

Wednesday
Numbers 27:1-11
Luke 11:33-36

The General Rule of Discipleship
*To witness to Jesus Christ in the world and to follow his teachings
through acts of compassion, justice, worship, and devotion under the guidance of the Holy Spirit.*

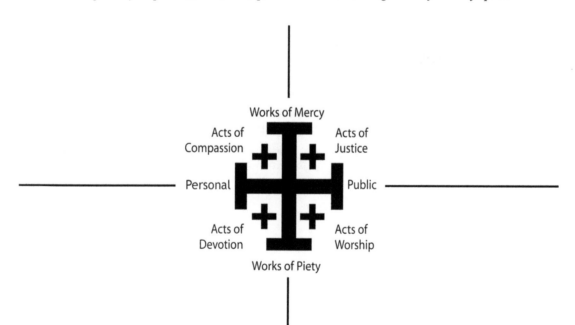

Works of Mercy

Acts of Compassion   Acts of Justice

Personal   Public

Acts of Devotion   Acts of Worship

Works of Piety

A Word from John Wesley

What is the difference then between the "righteousness which is of the law," and the "righteousness which is of faith?" Between the first covenant, or the covenant of works, and the second, the covenant of grace? The essential, unchangeable difference is this: the one supposes him to whom it is given to be already holy and happy, created in the image and enjoying the favour of God; and prescribes the condition whereon he may continue therein, in love and joy, life and immortality. The other supposes him to whom it is given to be now unholy and unhappy, fallen short of the glorious image of God, having the wrath of God abiding on him, and hastening, through sin, whereby his soul is dead, to bodily death, and death everlasting.

Sermon 6: "The Righteousness of Faith," § I.11

A Hymn from Charles Wesley

Come, sinners, to the gospel feast;
Let every soul be Jesu's guest;
Ye need not one be left behind,
For God hath bidden all mankind.

Sent by my Lord, on you I call;
The invitation is to all:
Come all the world; come, sinner, thou!
All things in Christ are ready now.

Come, all ye souls by sin oppressed,
Ye restless wanderers after rest;
Ye poor, and maimed, and halt, and blind,
In Christ a hearty welcome find.

A Collection of Hymns for the Use of The People Called Methodists (1781), #2:1-3

Prayers, Comments & Questions

God of grace and glory, you call us with your voice of flame to be your people, faithful and courageous. As your beloved Son embraced his mission in the waters of baptism, inspire us with the fire of your Spirit to join in his transforming work. We ask this in the name of our Savior Jesus Christ who lives and reigns for ever and ever. Amen.

Second Sunday After the Epiphany

Preparation for Sunday
Daily: Psalm 36:5-10

Thursday
Jeremiah 3:1-5
Acts 8:18-24

Friday
Jeremiah 3:19-25
1 Corinthians 7:1-7

Saturday
Jeremiah 4:1-4
Luke 11:14-23

Sunday
Isaiah 62:1-5
Psalm 36:5-10
1 Corinthians 12:1-11
John 2:1-11

Reflection on Sunday
Daily: Psalm 145

Monday
Isaiah 54:1-8
Romans 12:9-21

Tuesday
Song of Solomon 4:1-8
1 Corinthians 1:3-17

Wednesday
Song of Solomon 4:9—5:1
Luke 5:33-39

The General Rule of Discipleship
*To witness to Jesus Christ in the world and to follow his teachings
through acts of compassion, justice, worship, and devotion under the guidance of the Holy Spirit.*

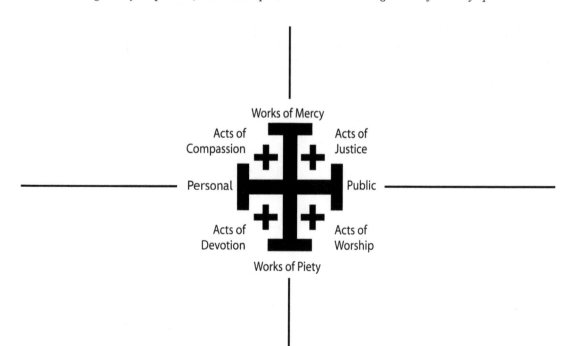

A Word from John Wesley

Dost thou now believe? Then "the love of God is" now "shed abroad in thy heart." Thou lovest him, because he first loved us. And because thou lovest God, thou lovest thy brother also. And being filled with "love, peace, joy," thou art also filled with "long-suffering, gentleness, fidelity, goodness, meekness, temperance," and all the other fruits of the same Spirit—in a word, with whatever dispositions are holy, are heavenly or divine. For while thou "beholdest with open (uncovered) face" (the veil now being taken away) "the glory of the Lord," his glorious love, and the glorious image wherein thou wast created, thou art "changed into the same image, from glory to glory, by the Spirit of the Lord."

Sermon 7: "The Way to the Kingdom," § II.12

A Hymn from Charles Wesley

Ho! every one that thirsts, draw nigh,
('Tis God invites the fallen race),
Mercy and free salvation buy;
Buy wine, and milk, and gospel-grace.

Come to the living waters, come!
Sinners, obey your Maker's call;
Return, ye weary wanderers home,
And find my grace is free for all.

See from the rock a fountain rise!
For you in healing streams it rolls;
Money ye need not bring, nor price,
Ye labouring, burdened, sin-sick souls.

(*Collection*—1781, #4: 1-3)

Prayers, Comments & Questions

O God of steadfast love, at the wedding in Cana your Son Jesus turned water into wine, delighting all who were there. Transform our hearts by your Spirit, that we may use our varied gifts to show forth the light of your love as one body in Christ. Amen.

Third Sunday After the Epiphany

Preparation for Sunday
Daily: Psalm 19

Thursday
Isaiah 61:1-7
Romans 7:1-6

Friday
Nehemiah 2:1-10
Romans 12:1-8

Saturday
Nehemiah 5:1-13
Luke 2:39-52

Sunday
Nehemiah 8:1-3, 5-6, 8-10
Psalm 19
1 Corinthians 12:12-31a
Luke 4:14-21

Reflection on Sunday
Daily: Psalm 119:89-96

Monday
Jeremiah 36:1-10
1 Corinthians 14:1-12

Tuesday
Jeremiah 36:11-26
2 Corinthians 7:2-12

Wednesday
Jeremiah 36:27-32
Luke 4:38-44

The General Rule of Discipleship
To witness to Jesus Christ in the world and to follow his teachings
through acts of compassion, justice, worship, and devotion under the guidance of the Holy Spirit.

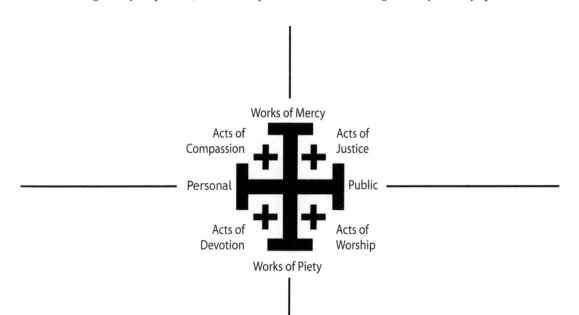

A Word from John Wesley

They now "walk after the Spirit" both in their hearts and lives. They are taught of him to love God and their neighbour, with a love which is as "a well of water, springing up into everlasting life." And by him they are led into every holy desire, into every divine and heavenly temper, till every thought which arises in their heart is holiness unto the Lord.

Sermon 8: "The First Fruits of the Spirit," § I.4

A Hymn from Charles Wesley

Thy faithfulness, Lord,
Each moment we find,
So true to thy word,
So loving and kind!
Thy mercy so tender
To all the lost race,
The foulest offender
May turn and find grace.

To save what was lost
From heaven he came.
Come, sinners, and trust
In Jesus's name.
He offers you pardon,
He bids you be free.
If sin is your burden,
O come unto me!

(*Collection*—1781, #5:1, 3)

Prayers, Comments & Questions

In you, O Lord our God, we find our joy, for through your law and your prophets you formed a people in mercy and freedom, in justice and righteousness. Pour your Spirit on us today, that we who are Christ's body may bear the good news of your ancient promises to all who seek you. Amen.

Fourth Sunday After the Epiphany

If this Sunday immediately precedes Ash Wednesday, the proper for Sunday and the readings for the surrounding days may be replaced, in those churches observing the Transfiguration on that Sunday, by the proper for the Last Sunday after the Epiphany and the readings for the days surrounding it.

Preparation for Sunday
Daily: Psalm 71:1-6

Thursday
2 Chronicles 34:1-7
Acts 10:44-48

Friday
2 Chronicles 35:20-27
Acts 19:1-10

Saturday
2 Chronicles 36:11-21
John 1:43-51

Sunday
Jeremiah 1:4-10
Psalm 71:1-6
1 Corinthians 13:1-13
Luke 4:21-30

Reflection on Sunday
Daily: Psalm 56

Monday
1 Kings 17:8-16
1 Corinthians 2:6-16

Tuesday
2 Kings 5:1-14
1 Corinthians 14:13-25

Wednesday
Jeremiah 1:11-19
Luke 19:41-44

The General Rule of Discipleship
*To witness to Jesus Christ in the world and to follow his teachings
through acts of compassion, justice, worship, and devotion under the guidance of the Holy Spirit.*

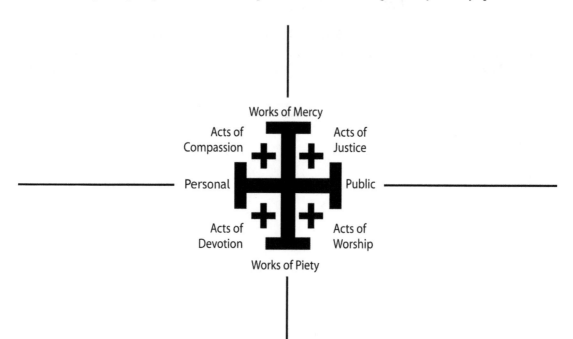

A Word from John Wesley

Art thou daily fighting against all sin? And daily more than conqueror? I acknowledge thee for a child of God. O stand fast in thy glorious liberty! Art thou fighting, but not conquering? Striving for the mastery, but not able to attain? Then thou art not yet a believer in Christ; but follow on, and thou shalt know the Lord. Art thou not fighting at all, but leading an easy, indolent, fashionable life! O how hast thou dared to name the name of Christ, only to make it a reproach among the Heathen? Awake, thou sleeper! Call upon thy God before the deep swallow thee up!

Sermon 9: "The Spirit of Bondage and of Adoption," § IV.1

A Hymn from Charles Wesley

Sinners, turn, why will you die?
God, your Maker, asks you why.
God, who did your being give,
Made you with himself to live;
He the fatal cause demands,
Asks the work of his own hands,
Why, you thankless creatures, why
Will you cross his love and die?

Sinners, turn, why will you die?
God, your Saviour, asks you why.
God, who did your souls retrieve,
Died himself that you might live.
Will you let him die in vain?
Crucify your Lord again?
Why, you ransomed sinners, why
Will you slight his grace and die?

(*Collection*—1781, #6:1, 2)

Prayers, Comments & Questions

O God of all the prophets, you knew us and chose us before you formed us in the womb. Fill us with faith that speaks your word, hope that does not disappoint, and love that bears all things for your sake, until that day when we shall know you fully, even as we are known by you. Amen.

Fifth Sunday After the Epiphany

If this Sunday immediately precedes Ash Wednesday, the proper for Sunday and the readings for the surrounding days may be replaced, in those churches observing the Transfiguration on that Sunday, by the proper for the Last Sunday after the Epiphany and the readings for the days surrounding it.

Preparation for Sunday
Daily: Psalm 138

Thursday
Numbers 20:22-29
Acts 9:19b-25

Friday
Numbers 27:12-23
Acts 9:26-31

Saturday
Judges 3:7-11
Luke 4:42-44

Sunday
Isaiah 6:1-13
Psalm 138
1 Corinthians 15:1-11
Luke 5:1-11

Reflection on Sunday
Daily: Psalm 115

Monday
Judges 5:1-11
1 Corinthians 14:26-40

Tuesday
1 Samuel 9:15—10:1b
1 Timothy 3:1-9

Wednesday
Isaiah 8:1-15
Luke 5:27-32

The General Rule of Discipleship
*To witness to Jesus Christ in the world and to follow his teachings
through acts of compassion, justice, worship, and devotion under the guidance of the Holy Spirit.*

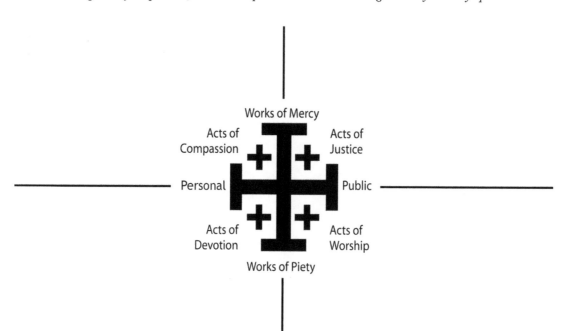

Works of Mercy

Acts of Compassion

Acts of Justice

Personal

Public

Acts of Devotion

Acts of Worship

Works of Piety

A Word from John Wesley

We must be holy of heart, and holy in life before we can be conscious that we are so; before we can have the testimony of our spirit, that we are inwardly and outwardly holy. But we must love God, before we can be holy at all; this being the root of all holiness. Now we cannot love God, till we know he loves us. "We love him, because he first loved us." And we cannot know his pardoning love to us, till his Spirit witnesses it to our spirit. Since, therefore, this testimony of his Spirit must precede the love of God and all holiness, of consequence it must precede our inward consciousness thereof, or the testimony of our spirit concerning them.

Sermon 10: "The Witness of the Spirit, I" § I.8

A Hymn from Charles Wesley

You, whom he ordained to be
Transcripts of the Trinity;
You, whom he in life doth hold,
You, for whom himself was sold,
You, on whom he still doth wait,
Whom he would again create;
Made by him, and purchased, why,
Why will you for ever die?

You, who own his record true,
You, his chosen people, you,
You, who call the Saviour Lord,
You, who read his written word,
You, who see the gospel light,
Claim a crown in Jesu's right;
Why will you, ye Christians, why
Will the house of Israel die?

(*Collection—1781, #7:3, 4*)

Prayers, Comments & Questions

Loving God, you have called forth disciples and prophets to live and speak your word. Give us ears to hear, lives to respond, and voices to proclaim the good news of salvation, which we know in our Savior Jesus Christ, who lives and reigns with you and the Holy Spirit, one God, now and forever. Amen.

Sixth Sunday After the Epiphany

If this Sunday immediately precedes Ash Wednesday, the proper for Sunday and the readings for the surrounding days may be replaced, in those churches observing the Transfiguration on that Sunday, by the proper for the Last Sunday after the Epiphany and the readings for the days surrounding it.

Preparation for Sunday
Daily: Psalm 1

Thursday
Jeremiah 13:12-19
Acts 13:26-34

Friday
Jeremiah 13:20-27
1 Peter 1:17—2:1

Saturday
Jeremiah 17:1-4
Luke 11:24-28

Sunday
Jeremiah 17:5-10
Psalm 1
1 Corinthians 15:12-20
Luke 6:17-26

Reflection on Sunday
Daily: Psalm 120

Monday
2 Kings 24:18—25:21
1 Corinthians 15:20-34

Tuesday
Ezra 1:1-11
2 Corinthians 1:12-19

Wednesday
Jeremiah 22:11-17
Luke 11:37-52

The General Rule of Discipleship
*To witness to Jesus Christ in the world and to follow his teachings
through acts of compassion, justice, worship, and devotion under the guidance of the Holy Spirit.*

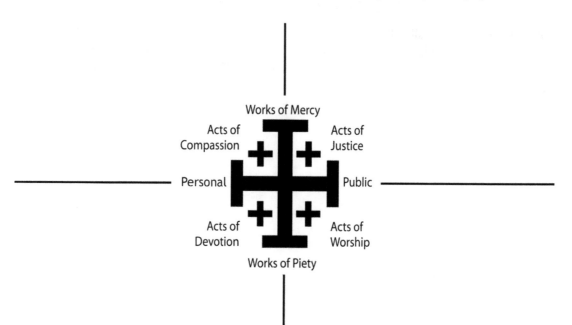

A Word from John Wesley

I observed many years ago, "It is hard to find words in the language of men, to explain the deep things of God. Indeed there are none that will adequately express what the Spirit of God works in his children. But perhaps one might say, (desiring any who are taught of God, to correct, soften, or strengthen the expression,) By the testimony of the Spirit, I mean, an inward impression on the soul whereby the Spirit of God immediately and directly witnesses to my spirit, that I am a child of God; that Jesus Christ hath loved me, and given himself for me; that all my sins are blotted out, and I, even I, am reconciled to God."

Sermon 11: "The Witness of the Spirit, II" § II.2

A Hymn from Charles Wesley

Turn, he cries, ye sinners, turn;
By his life your God hath sworn
He would have you turn and live,
He would all the world receive;
If your death were his delight,
Would he you to life invite?
Would he ask, obtest, and cry,
Why will you resolve to die?

Sinners, turn, while God is near;
Dare not think him insincere;
Now, even now, your Saviour stands,
All day long he spreads his hands;
Cries, Ye will not happy be;
No, ye will not come to me!
Me, who life to none deny;
Why will you resolve to die?

(*Collection—1781, #8: 2, 3*)

Prayers, Comments & Questions

God, you root those who trust in you by streams of healing water. Release us from the bonds of disease, free us from the power of evil, and turn us from falsehood and illusion, that we may find the blessing of new life in you through the power of Christ. Amen.

Seventh Sunday After the Epiphany

If this Sunday immediately precedes Ash Wednesday, the proper for Sunday and the readings for the surrounding days may be replaced, in those churches observing the Transfiguration on that Sunday, by the proper for the Last Sunday after the Epiphany and the readings for the days surrounding it.

Preparation for Sunday
Daily: Psalm 37:1-11, 39-40

Thursday
Genesis 43:16-34
Romans 8:1-11

Friday
Genesis 44:1-17
1 John 2:12-17

Saturday
Genesis 44:18-34
Luke 12:57-59

Sunday
Genesis 45:3-11, 15
Psalm 37:1-11, 39-40
1 Cor. 15:35-38, 42-50
Luke 6:27-38

Reflection on Sunday
Daily: Psalm 38

Monday
Genesis 33:1-17
1 Corinthians 11:2-16

Tuesday
1 Samuel 24:1-22
1 Corinthians 11:17-22, 27-33

Wednesday
Leviticus 5:1-13
Luke 17:1-4

The General Rule of Discipleship
*To witness to Jesus Christ in the world and to follow his teachings
through acts of compassion, justice, worship, and devotion under the guidance of the Holy Spirit.*

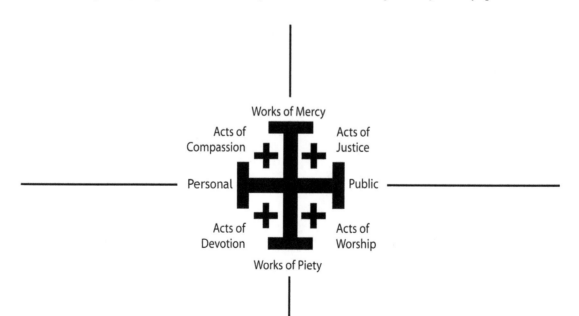

A Word from John Wesley

But whoever desires to have a conscience thus void of offence, let him see that he lay the right foundation. Let him remember, "other foundation" of this "can no man lay, than that which is laid, even Jesus Christ." And let him also be mindful, that no man buildeth on him but by a living faith; that no man is a partaker of Christ, until he can clearly testify, "The life which I now live, I live by faith in the Son of God;" in him who is now *revealed* in my heart; who "loved me, and gave himself for me." Faith alone is that evidence, that conviction, that demonstration of things invisible, whereby the eyes of our understanding being opened, and divine light poured in upon them, we "see the wondrous things of God's law;" the excellency and purity of it; the height, and depth, and length, and breadth thereof, and of every commandment contained therein.

Sermon 12: "The Witness of Our Own Spirit," ¶ 8

A Hymn from Charles Wesley

Sinners, obey the gospel word;
Haste to the supper of my Lord;
Be wise to know your gracious day!
All things are ready, come away!

Ready the Father is to own,
And kiss his late-returning son;
Ready your loving Saviour stands,
And spreads for you his bleeding hands.

Ready the Spirit of his love
Just now the stony to remove;
T'apply, and witness with the blood,
And wash, and seal the sons of God.

Ready for you the angels wait,
To triumph in your blest estate;
Tuning their harps they long to praise
The wonders of redeeming grace.

(*Collection—1781, #9:1-4*)

Prayers, Comments & Questions

O perfect Love, whose compassionate power transforms sin into health and temporal dust into eternal glory: Grant us a gracious faith, so that like Joseph, when he was sold into slavery, we may face our trials with confidence, and become a blessing to friend and enemy alike in Jesus' name. Amen.

Eighth Sunday After the Epiphany

If this Sunday immediately precedes Ash Wednesday, the proper for Sunday and the readings for the surrounding days may be replaced, in those churches observing the Transfiguration on that Sunday, by the proper for the Last Sunday after the Epiphany and the readings for the days surrounding it.

Preparation for Sunday
Daily: Psalm 92:1-4, 12-15

Thursday
Proverbs 13:1-12
Romans 5:12—6:2

Friday
Proverbs 15:1-9
1 Thessalonians 4:13-18

Saturday
Isaiah 30:8-17
John 16:1-4a

Sunday
Isaiah 55:10-13
Psalm 92:1-4, 12-15
1 Corinthians 15:51-58
Luke 6:39-49

Reflection on Sunday
Daily: Psalm 1

Monday
Jeremiah 24:1-10
1 Corinthians 16:1-12

Tuesday
Jeremiah 29:10-19
1 Corinthians 16:13-24

Wednesday
Proverbs 5:1-23
Luke 14:34-35

The General Rule of Discipleship
*To witness to Jesus Christ in the world and to follow his teachings
through acts of compassion, justice, worship, and devotion under the guidance of the Holy Spirit.*

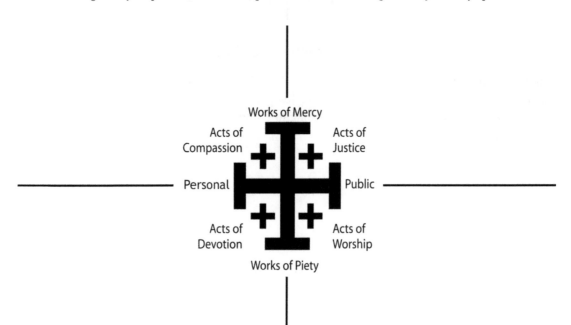

A Word from John Wesley

We are then simple of heart, when the eye of our mind is singly fixed on God; when in all things we aim at God alone, as our God, our portion, our strength, our happiness, our exceeding great reward, our all, in time and eternity. This is simplicity; when a steady view, a single intention of promoting his glory, of doing and suffering his blessed will, runs through our whole soul, fills all our heart, and is the constant spring of all our thoughts, desires, and purposes.

Sermon 12: "The Witness of Our Own Spirit," ¶ 11

A Hymn from Charles Wesley

Jesu, the sinner's friend, to thee
Lost and undone for aid I flee,
Weary of Earth, myself, and sin
Open thine arms, and take me in.

Pity and heal my sin-sick soul,
'Tis thou alone canst make me whole,
Fallen, till in me thine image shine,
And cursed I am till thou art mine.

Hear, Jesu, hear my helpless cry,
O save a wretch condemned to die!
The sentence in myself I feel,
And all my nature teems with hell.

Hymns and Sacred Poems (1739), p. 92

Prayers, Comments & Questions

From your mouth, O God, come mercy and righteousness, and out of the abundance of your heart you have given us your Word made flesh, Jesus the Christ. Pour out your Spirit of integrity upon us, that all we say and do may befit a people made in your image and baptized into the dying and rising of your Son. Amen.

Ninth Sunday After the Epiphany

If this Sunday immediately precedes Ash Wednesday, the proper for Sunday and the readings for the surrounding days may be replaced, in those churches observing the Transfiguration on that Sunday, by the proper for the Last Sunday after the Epiphany and the readings for the days surrounding it.

Preparation for Sunday
Daily: Psalm 96:1-9

Thursday
1 Kings 6:23-38
2 Corinthians 5:11-17

Friday
1 Kings 8:14-21
2 Corinthians 11:1-6

Saturday
1 Kings 8:31-40
Luke 4:31-37

Sunday
1 Kings 8:22-23, 41-43
Psalm 96:1-9
Galatians 1:1-12
Luke 7:1-10

Reflection on Sunday
Daily: Psalm 5

Monday
Jonah 4:1-11
Acts 8:26-40

Tuesday
Nehemiah 1:1-11
Acts 3:1-10

Wednesday
Isaiah 56:1-8
Mark 7:24-30

The General Rule of Discipleship
To witness to Jesus Christ in the world and to follow his teachings through acts of compassion, justice, worship, and devotion under the guidance of the Holy Spirit.

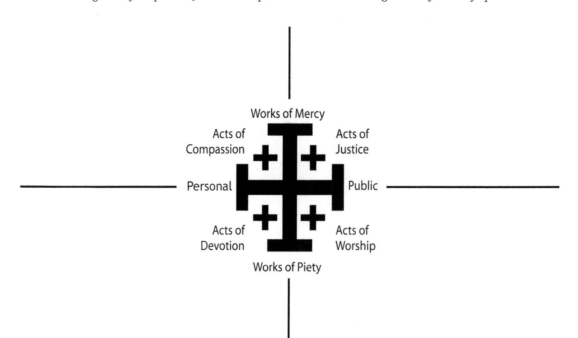

Works of Mercy

Acts of Compassion   Acts of Justice

Personal   Public

Acts of Devotion   Acts of Worship

Works of Piety

A Word from John Wesley

It could not be that ever he should attain to this but by the "excellent knowledge of Jesus Christ" our Lord; or, "by the grace of God,"—another expression of nearly the same import. By "the grace of God" is sometimes to be understood that free love, that unmerited mercy, by which I a sinner, through the merits of Christ, am now reconciled to God. But in this place it rather means that power of God the Holy Ghost, which "worketh in us both to will and to do of his good pleasure." As soon as ever the grace of God in the former sense, his pardoning love, is manifested to our souls, the grace of God in the latter sense, the power of his Spirit, takes place therein. And now we can perform, through God, what to man was impossible.

Sermon 12: "The Witness of Our Own Spirit," ¶ 15

A Hymn from Charles Wesley

Long have I vainly hoped and strove
To force my hardness into love,
To give thee all thy laws require;
And labored in the purging fire.

A thousand specious arts essayed,
Called the deep *Mystic* to my aid:
His boasted skill the brute refined,
But left the subtler fiend behind.

Frail, dark, impure, I still remain,
Nor hope to break my nature's chain:
The fond self-emptying scheme is past,
And lo! Constrained I yield at last.

At last I own it cannot be
That I should fit myself for thee:
Here then to thee, I all resign,
Thine is the work, and only thine.

Hymns and Sacred Poems (1739), pp. 93–94

Prayers, Comments & Questions

The greatness of your deeds, Lord God, declares your love for all people and shows forth the glory of your name. Teach us to welcome both our neighbor and the stranger in our midst, that all may know the healing touch of your Son, who announces the good news of salvation in word and deed. Amen.

Last Sunday After the Epiphany: Transfiguration Sunday

Preparation for Sunday
Daily: Psalm 99

Thursday
Deuteronomy 9:1-5
Acts 3:11-16

Friday
Deuteronomy 9:6-14
Acts 10:1-8

Saturday
Deuteronomy 9:15-24
Luke 10:21-24

Sunday
Exodus 34:29-35
Psalm 99
2 Corinthians 3:12—4:2
Luke 9:28-43

Reflection on Sunday
Daily: Psalm 35:11-28

Monday
Exodus 35:1-29
Acts 10:9-23a

Tuesday
Ezekiel 1:1—2:1
Acts 10:23b-33

Ash Wednesday
Isaiah 58:1-12
Psalm 51:1-17
2 Corinthians 5:20b—6:10
Matthew 6:1-6, 16-21

The General Rule of Discipleship
*To witness to Jesus Christ in the world and to follow his teachings
through acts of compassion, justice, worship, and devotion under the guidance of the Holy Spirit.*

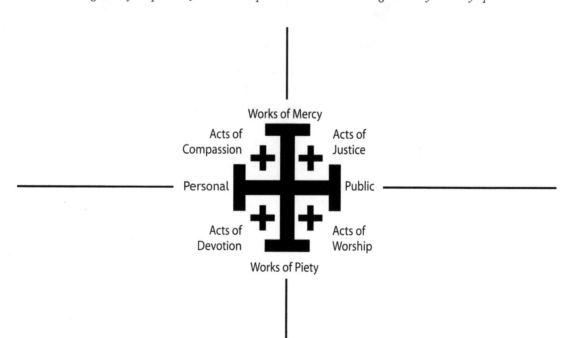

Works of Mercy

Acts of Compassion

Acts of Justice

Personal

Public

Acts of Devotion

Acts of Worship

Works of Piety

A Word from John Wesley

Thus it is, that in the children of God, repentance and faith exactly answer each other. By repentance we feel the sin remaining in our hearts, and cleaving to our words and actions: by faith, we receive the power of God in Christ, purifying our hearts, and cleansing our hands. By repentance, we are still sensible that we deserve punishment for all our tempers, and words, and actions: by faith, we are conscious that our Advocate with the Father is continually pleading for us, and thereby continually turning aside all condemnation and punishment from us.

Sermon 14: "The Repentance of Believers," § II.6

A Hymn from Charles Wesley

Sinners, turn, why will you die?
God the Spirit asks you why.
He, who all your lives hath strove,
Wooed you to embrace his love.
Will you not the grace receive?
Will you still refuse to live?
Why, you long-sought sinners, why
Will you grieve your God and die?

Dead already, dead within,
Spiritually dead in sin,
Dead to God while here you breathe,
Pant you after second death?
Will you still in sin remain,
Greedy of eternal pain?
O you dying sinners, why,
Why will you for ever die?

(*Collection*—1781, #6:3, 4)

Prayers, Comments & Questions

Transfiguration Sunday

Holy God, mighty and immortal, you are beyond our knowing, yet we see your glory in the face of Jesus Christ, whose compassion illumines the world. Transform us into the likeness of the love of Christ, who renewed our humanity so that we may share in his divinity, the same Jesus Christ, our Lord, who lives and reigns with you and the Holy Spirit. Amen.

Ash Wednesday

O God, you delight not in pomp and show, but in a humble and contrite heart. Overturn our love of worldly possessions and fix our hearts more firmly on you, that, having nothing, we may yet possess everything, a treasure stored up for us in heaven. Amen.

Lent

Forming Disciples Who Live as Jesus Lived

The primary purpose of Lent, from its beginnings, has been to provide a period of intense formation for those preparing to take on the covenant of baptism with the baptized, with baptism celebrated at Easter. Over time, as the early church's extensive three-year system of formation (called the catechumenate) fell into disuse, Lent became in practice primarily a time for penitence and increased acts of self-discipline, as well as, in some ways, particularly among Protestants, a kind of "extended Holy Week" for contemplating the suffering of Jesus.

With the renewal of the Christian Year brought about for Roman Catholics in Vatican II (early 1960s) and for Protestants coinciding with the development of the Revised Common Lectionary (1992), more and more Western Christians have recovered the idea, if not entirely the practices, of Lent as a season of preparation for baptism, reconciliation for the estranged, and final preparation for confirmation or reaffirmation by those baptized who are deemed ready to take the vows of baptism for themselves for the first time or in a deeper way.

Consequently, the readings you will experience on Sundays and weekdays during Lent are much more about how Jesus teaches his disciples to follow him and not about the sufferings of Jesus or his execution per se. And every year the Sunday readings correspond with key elements of the baptismal vows. If your congregation is not already providing accountable small groups to read and explore the implications of these readings, Sunday and/or daily, for living as the baptized, let me encourage you to gather a few Christian friends and create your own. Consider meeting face to face at least once weekly.

When you gather, read one of the Gospel readings aloud three times, *lectio continua* style, paying notice the first time to what catches your attention, the second to what the thing that caught your attention is calling you to do, and the third to how you will respond in obedience to do it. Then, share what you have gleaned from your reading with others in your small group. Decide how you will help one another be obedient to what each of you has heard during the coming week.

Rev. Taylor Burton-Edwards

First Sunday in Lent

Preparation for Sunday
Daily: Psalm 91:1-2, 9-16

Thursday
Exodus 5:10-23
Acts 7:30-34

Friday
Exodus 6:1-13
Acts 7:35-42

Saturday
Ecclesiastes 3:1-8
John 12:27-36

Sunday
Deuteronomy 26:1-11
Psalm 91:1-2, 9-16
Romans 10:8b-13
Luke 4:1-13

Reflection on Sunday
Daily: Psalm 17

Monday
1 Chronicles 21:1-17
1 John 2:1-6

Tuesday
Zechariah 3:1-10
2 Peter 2:4-21

Wednesday
Job 1:1-22
Luke 21:34—22:6

The General Rule of Discipleship
*To witness to Jesus Christ in the world and to follow his teachings
through acts of compassion, justice, worship, and devotion under the guidance of the Holy Spirit.*

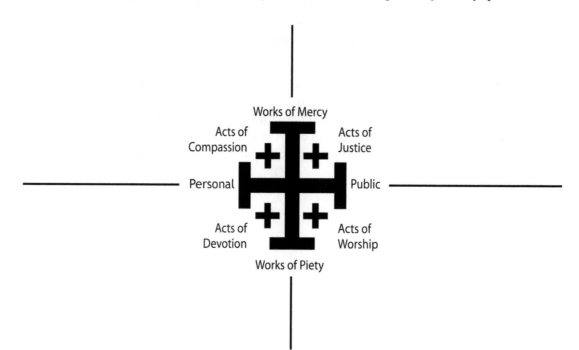

A Word from John Wesley

The person by whom God will judge the world, is his only-begotten Son, whose "goings forth are from everlasting;" "who is God over all, blessed for ever." Unto him, being "the outbeaming of his Father's glory, the express image of his person" (Heb. 1:3), the Father "hath committed all judgement, because he is the Son of Man" (John 5:22, 27); because, though he was "in the form of God, and thought it not robbery to be equal with God, yet he emptied himself, taking upon him the form of a servant, being made in the likeness of men" (Phil. 2:6, 7); yea, because, "being found in fashion as a man, he humbled himself" yet farther, "becoming obedient unto death, even the death of the cross."

Sermon 15: The Great Assize, § II.1

A Hymn from Charles Wesley

Let the beasts their breath resign,
Strangers to the life divine;
Who their God can never know,
Let their spirit downward go.
You for higher ends were born,
You may all to God return,
Dwell with him above the sky:
Why will you for ever die?

You, on whom he favours showers,
You, possessed of nobler powers,
You, of reason's powers possessed,
You, with will and memory blest:
You, with finer sense endued,
Creatures capable of God;
Noblest of his creatures, why,
Why will you for ever die?

(*Collection*—1781, #7:1 & 2)

Prayers, Comments & Questions

God of deliverance and freedom, you taught the people of Israel to acknowledge that all things come from your bountiful hand. Deepen our faith so that we may resist temptation and, in the midst of trial, proclaim that Jesus Christ is Lord, now and forever. Amen.

Second Sunday in Lent

Preparation for Sunday
Daily: Psalm 27

Thursday
Genesis 13:1-7, 14-18
Philippians 3:2-12

Friday
Genesis 14:17-24
Philippians 3:17-20

Saturday
Psalm 118:26-29
Matthew 23:37-39

Sunday
Genesis 15:1-12, 17-18
Psalm 27
Philippians 3:17—4:1
Luke 13:31-35

Reflection on Sunday
Daily: Psalm 105:1-15, 42

Monday
Exodus 33:1-6
Romans 4:1-12

Tuesday
Numbers 14:10b-24
1 Corinthians 10:1-13

Wednesday
2 Chronicles 20:1-22
Luke 13:22-31

The General Rule of Discipleship
To witness to Jesus Christ in the world and to follow his teachings
through acts of compassion, justice, worship, and devotion under the guidance of the Holy Spirit.

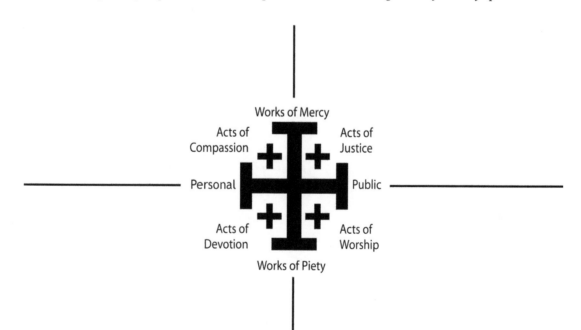

A Word from John Wesley

According to the decision of holy writ all who desire the grace of God are to wait for it in the means which he hath ordained; in using, not in laying them aside. And, First, all who desire the grace of God are to wait for it in the way of prayer. This is the express direction of our Lord himself. In his Sermon upon the Mount, after explaining at large wherein religion consists, and describing the main branches of it, he adds, "Ask, and it shall be given you; seek, and ye shall find; knock, and it shall be opened unto you: For everyone that asketh receiveth; and he that seeketh findeth; and to him that knocketh it shall be opened." (Matt. 7:7, 8)

Sermon 16: "The Means of Grace," §III.1

A Hymn from Charles Wesley

You, whom he ordained to be
Transcripts of the Trinity;
You, whom he in life doth hold,
You, for whom himself was sold,
You, on whom he still doth wait,
Whom he would again create;
Made by him, and purchased, why,
Why will you for ever die?

You, who own his record true,
You, his chosen people, you,
You, who call the Saviour Lord,
You, who read his written word,
You, who see the gospel light,
Claim a crown in Jesu's right;
Why will you, ye Christians, why
Will the house of Israel die?

(*Collection*—1781, #7:3, 4)

Prayers, Comments & Questions

Hope beyond all human hope, you promised descendants as numerous as the stars to old Abraham and barren Sarah. You promise light and salvation in the midst of darkness and despair, and promise redemption to a world that will not listen. Gather us to yourself in tenderness, open our ears to listen to your word, and teach us to live faithfully as people confident of the fulfillment of your promises. We ask this in the name of Jesus Christ. Amen.

Third Sunday in Lent

Preparation for Sunday
Daily: Psalm 63:1-8

Thursday
Daniel 3:19-30
Revelation 2:8-11

Friday
Daniel 12:1-4
Revelation 3:1-6

Saturday
Isaiah 5:1-7
Luke 6:43-45

Sunday
Isaiah 55:1-9
Psalm 63:1-8
1 Corinthians 10:1-13
Luke 13:1-9

Reflection on Sunday
Daily: Psalm 39

Monday
Jeremiah 11:1-17
Romans 2:1-11

Tuesday
Ezekiel 17:1-10
Romans 2:12-16

Wednesday
Numbers 13:17-27
Luke 13:18-21

The General Rule of Discipleship
To witness to Jesus Christ in the world and to follow his teachings
through acts of compassion, justice, worship, and devotion under the guidance of the Holy Spirit.

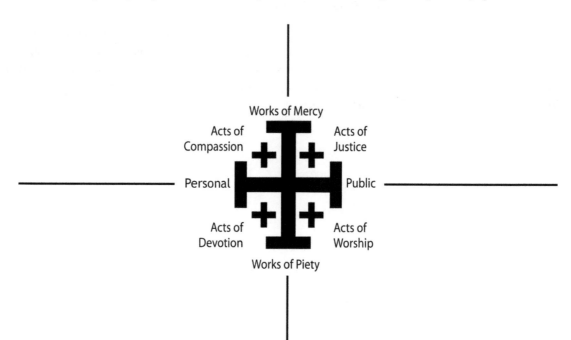

A Word from John Wesley

To be more particular: Circumcision of heart implies humility, faith, hope, and charity. Humility, a right judgment of ourselves, cleanses our minds from those high conceits of our own perfection, from that undue opinion of our own abilities and attainments, which are the genuine fruit of a corrupted nature. This entirely cuts off that vain thought, "I am rich, and wise, and have need of nothing;" and convinces us that we are by nature wretched, and poor, and miserable, and blind, and naked.

Sermon 17: "Circumcision of the Heart," § I.2

A Hymn from Charles Wesley

Sinners, obey the gospel word;
Haste to the supper of my Lord;
Be wise to know your gracious day!
All things are ready, come away!

Ready the Father is to own,
And kiss his late-returning son;
Ready your loving Saviour stands,
And spreads for you his bleeding hands.

Ready the Spirit of his love
Just now the stony to remove;
T'apply, and witness with the blood,
And wash, and seal the sons of God.

Ready for you the angels wait,
To triumph in your blest estate;
Tuning their harps, they long to praise
The wonders of redeeming grace.

(*Collection*—1781, #9:1-4)

Prayers, Comments & Questions

God of infinite goodness, throughout the ages you have persevered in claiming and reclaiming your people. Renew for us your call to repentance, surround us with witnesses to aid us in our journey, and grant us the time to fashion our lives anew, through Jesus Christ our Savior. Amen.

Fourth Sunday in Lent

Preparation for Sunday
Daily: Psalm 32

Thursday
Joshua 4:1-13
2 Corinthians 4:16—5:5

Friday
Joshua 4:14-24
2 Corinthians 5:6-15

Saturday
Exodus 32:7-14
Luke 15:1-10

Sunday
Joshua 5:9-12
Psalm 32
2 Corinthians 5:16-21
Luke 15:1-3, 11b-32

Reflection on Sunday
Daily: Psalm 53

Monday
Leviticus 23:26-41
Revelation 19:1-8

Tuesday
Leviticus 25:1-19
Revelation 19:9-10

Wednesday
2 Kings 4:1-7
Luke 9:10-17

The General Rule of Discipleship
*To witness to Jesus Christ in the world and to follow his teachings
through acts of compassion, justice, worship, and devotion under the guidance of the Holy Spirit.*

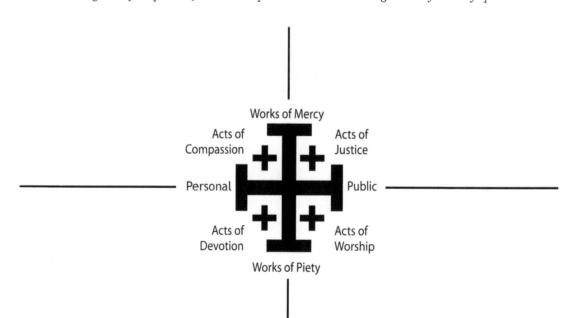

A Word from John Wesley

A Second fruit then of the love of God (so far as it can be distinguished from it) is universal obedience to him we love, and conformity to his will; obedience to all the commands of God, internal and external; obedience of the heart and of the life; in every temper, and in all manner of conversation. And one of the tempers most obviously implied herein, is, the being "zealous of good works;" the hungering and thirsting to do good, in every possible kind, unto all men; the rejoicing to "spend and be spent for them," for every child of man; not looking for any recompence in this world, but only in the resurrection of the just.

Sermon 18: "The Marks of the New Birth," § III.5

A Hymn from Charles Wesley

The Father, Son, and Holy Ghost
Is ready with their shining host;
All heaven is ready to resound:
"The dead's alive! The lost is found."

Come then, ye sinners, to your Lord,
Through Christ to paradise restored;
His proffered benefits embrace,
The plenitude of gospel grace:

A pardon written with his blood,
The favour and the peace of God;
The seeing eye, the feeling sense,
The mystic joys of penitence;

The godly fear, the pleasing smart,
The meltings of a broken heart;
The tears that tell your sins forgiven;
The sighs that waft your souls to heaven;

(*Collection*—1781, #9:5-8)

Prayers, Comments & Questions

God of patient love, you await the return of the wayward and wandering and eagerly embrace them in pardon. Through baptism you have clothed us with the glory of Christ and restored our inheritance: give us generous hearts to welcome all who seek a place at the table of your unconditional love. We ask this through Jesus Christ our Lord. Amen.

Fifth Sunday in Lent

Preparation for Sunday
Daily: Psalm 126

Thursday
Isaiah 43:1-7
Philippians 2:19-24

Friday
Isaiah 43:8-15
Philippians 2:25—3:1

Saturday
Exodus 12:21-27
John 11:45-57

Sunday
Isaiah 43:16-21
Psalm 126
Philippians 3:4b-14
John 12:1-8

Reflection on Sunday
Daily: Psalm 20

Monday
Exodus 40:1-15
Hebrews 10:19-25

Tuesday
Judges 9:7-15
1 John 2:18-28

Wednesday
Habakkuk 3:2-15
Luke 18:31-34

The General Rule of Discipleship
*To witness to Jesus Christ in the world and to follow his teachings
through acts of compassion, justice, worship, and devotion under the guidance of the Holy Spirit.*

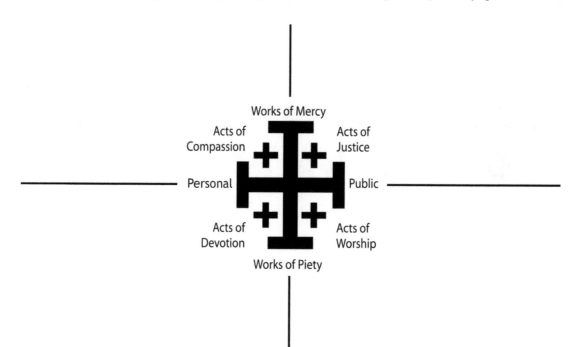

A Word from John Wesley

But when he is born of God, born of the Spirit, how is the manner of his existence changed! His whole soul is now sensible of God, and he can say, by sure experience, "Thou art about my bed, and about my path;" I feel thee in all my ways: "Thou besettest me behind and before, and layest thy hand upon me." The Spirit or breath of God is immediately inspired, breathed into the new-born soul; and the same breath which comes from, returns to, God: As it is continually received by faith, so it is continually rendered back by love, by prayer, and praise, and thanksgiving; love and praise, and prayer being the breath of every soul which is truly born of God.

Sermon 19: "The Great Privilege of Those That Are Born of God," § I.8

A Hymn from Charles Wesley

Come, ye that love the Lord,
And let your joys be known;
Join in a song with sweet accord
While you surround his throne.
Let those refuse to sing
Who never knew our God,
But servants of the heavenly king
May speak their joys abroad.

The God that rules on high,
That all the earth surveys,
That rides upon the stormy sky,
And calms the roaring seas;
This awful God is ours,
Our Father and our love;
He will send down his heavenly powers
To carry us above.

(*Collection*—1781, #12:1 & 2)

Prayers, Comments & Questions

Creator God, you prepare a new way in the wilderness and your grace waters the desert. Help us to recognize your hand working miracles beyond our imagining. Open our hearts to be transformed by the new thing you are doing, so that our lives may proclaim the extravagance of your love for all, and its presence in Jesus Christ. Amen.

Sixth Sunday in Lent: Passion/Palm Sunday

Preparation for Sunday
Daily: Psalm 31:9-16

Thursday
Isaiah 53:10-12
Hebrews 2:1-9

Friday
Isaiah 54:9-10
Hebrews 2:10-18

Saturday
Leviticus 23:1-8
Luke 22:1-13

Sunday
Liturgy of the Palms
Psalm 118:1-2, 19-29
Luke 19:28-40

Liturgy of the Passion
Isaiah 50:4-9a
Psalm 31:9-16
Philippians 2:5-11
Luke 22:14—23:56

The General Rule of Discipleship
To witness to Jesus Christ in the world and to follow his teachings
through acts of compassion, justice, worship, and devotion under the guidance of the Holy Spirit.

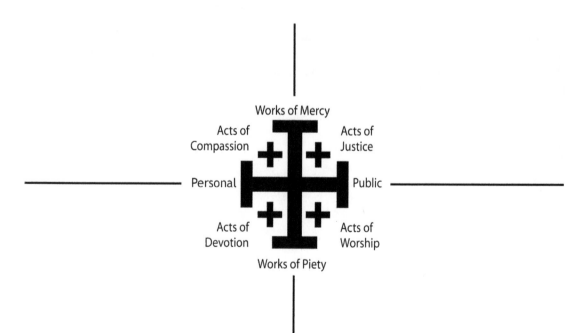

A Word from John Wesley

But in what sense is this righteousness imputed to believers? In this: all believers are forgiven and accepted, not for the sake of anything in them, or of anything that ever was, that is, or ever can be done by them, but wholly and solely for the sake of what Christ hath done and suffered for them. I say again, not for the sake of anything in them, or done by them, of their own righteousness or works: "Not for works of righteousness which we have done, but of his own mercy he saved us."

Sermon 20: "The Lord Our Righteousness," § II.5

A Hymn from Charles Wesley

Thou, Jesu, art our King,
Thy ceaseless praise we sing:
Praise shall our glad tongue employ,
Praise o'erflow our grateful soul,
While we vital breath enjoy,
While eternal ages roll.

Thou art the eternal light,
That shinest in deepest night.
Wondering gazed the angelic train
While thou bow'dst the heavens beneath,
God with God wert man with man,
Man to save from endless death

Thou for our pain didst mourn,
Thou hast our sickness born:
All our sins on thee were laid;
Thou with unexampled grace
All the mighty debt hast paid
Due from Adam's helpless race.

(*Hymns and Sacred Poems*—1739, p. 175)

Prayers, Comments & Questions

Compassionate God, your love finds full expression in the gift of Jesus Christ your Son, who willingly met betrayal and death to set us free from sin. Give us courage to live obediently in these days until we greet the glory of our risen Savior. Amen.

Holy Week

The Cost of Discipleship and Salvation

Lent moves into Holy Week beginning with Passion/Palm Sunday. This is the time we remember the final week of Jesus in Jerusalem, his last actions with his disciples, his arrest, his trial, his torture, and his execution. The daily readings (Monday through Saturday) are the same all three years, established by long tradition. And these are readings intended to be read and reflected upon in gathered community. Many congregations will have planned gatherings for worship on Maundy Thursday and Good Friday. Fewer may be likely to gather for the solemn vigil of Holy Saturday morning or the other weekdays.

The formational power of this week is greatly enhanced if you do gather every day in some way. Perhaps you may find a time each evening to meet in homes; or a "third place"; or perhaps you may decide to gather "virtually," through an online venue such as Skype, Facebook, or Twitter. While during Lent the focus of the readings was to commit to what you might do, during Holy Week the purpose is simply to let them sink in and allow the readings to work their work in your gathered community. Read the scriptures. Pray for the church and the world. Bid one another the peace of Christ. And continue to watch and pray for what the Spirit will put to death and bring to new life in each of you.

Rev. Taylor Burton-Edwards

Monday

Isaiah 42:1-9
Psalm 36:5-11
Hebrews 9:11-15
John 12:1-11

Collect for Monday of Holy Week

God of steadfast love, light of the blind and liberator of the oppressed, we see your holy purpose in the tender compassion of Jesus, who calls us into new and living friendship with you. May we, who take shelter in the shadow of your wings, be filled with the grace of his tender caring; may we, who stumble in selfish darkness, see your glory in the light of his self-giving. We ask this through him whose suffering is victorious, Jesus Christ our Savior. Amen.

Tuesday

Isaiah 49:1-7
Psalm 71:1-14
1 Corinthians 1:18-31
John 12:20-36

Collect for Tuesday of Holy Week

Holy and immortal God, from earliest times you have named us and called us into discipleship. Teach us to follow the One whose light scatters the darkness of our world, that we may walk as children of the light. Amen.

Wednesday

Isaiah 50:4-9a
Psalm 70
Hebrews 12:1-3
John 13:21-32

Collect for Wednesday of Holy Week

Troubled God, in every generation you call your people to contend against the brutality of sin and betrayal. Keep us steadfast even in our fear and uncertainty, that we may follow where Jesus has led the way. Amen.

The Three Days

Holy Thursday

Exodus 12:1-14
Psalm 116:1-2, 12-19
1 Corinthians 11:23-26
John 13:1-17, 31b-35

Collect for Holy Thursday

Eternal God, in the sharing of a meal your Son established a new covenant for all people, and in the washing of feet he showed us the dignity of service. Grant that by the power of your Holy Spirit these signs of our life in faith may speak again to our hearts, feed our spirits, and refresh our bodies. Amen.

Good Friday

Isaiah 52:13—53:12
Psalm 22
Hebrews 10:16-25
John 18:1—19:42

Collect for Good Friday

Grieving God, on the cross your Son embraced death even as he had embraced life: faithfully and with good courage. Grant that we who have been born out of his wounded side may hold fast to our faith in him exalted and may find mercy in all times of need. Amen.

Holy Saturday

Job 14:1-14
Psalm 31:1-4, 15-16
1 Peter 4:1-8
John 19:38-42

Collect for Holy Saturday

Eternal God, rock and refuge: with roots grown old in the earth, river beds run dry, and flowers withered in the field, we wait for revival and release. Abide with us until we come alive in the sunrise of your glory. Amen.

Hymn for Holy Week

O Love divine! What hast thou done!
Th'immortal God hath died for me!
The Father's co-eternal Son
Bore all my sins upon the tree:
Th'immortal God for me hath died!
My Lord, my Love, is crucified.

Behold him, all ye that pass by,
The bleeding Prince of life and peace!
Come see, ye worms, your Maker die,
And say, was ever grief like his?
Come, feel with me his blood applied:
My Lord, my Love, is crucified.

Is crucified for me and you,
To bring us rebels back to God;
Believe, believe the record true,
Ye all are bought with Jesu's blood:
Pardon for all flows from his side:
My Lord, my Love, is crucified.

Then let us sit beneath his cross,
And gladly catch the healing stream,
All things for him account bur loss,
And give up all our hearts to him;
Of nothing think or speak beside,
"My Lord, my Love, is crucified."

(*Collection*—1781, #27, 1-4)

Easter Season

Teaching and Preparing to Unleash Salvation

The first service of Easter is full of readings! This is the Great Vigil of Easter, offered after sundown on Saturday night. It is a powerful service of Fire, Word, Water, and Table. We light the new fire, signifying the light of Christ overcoming the world. We rehearse the story of God's salvation, from creation and exodus to the resurrection of Christ. We exult in Alleluias. We baptize those who have been preparing during Lent and vigiling in prayer with us during Holy Week. And we celebrate the feast of our redemption around the Lord's Table. If your congregation does not yet celebrate this amazing and ancient Christian service, find one that does (most Episcopal, Roman Catholic, and many Lutheran congregations will!) and take folks with you, including your pastor, so they may see, hear, smell, taste, and touch, and perhaps develop plans to bring others or create one for your congregation next year.

Easter, the Season of the Passover of our Lord, begins with a bang! And it concludes with another one, fifty days later at Pentecost, when we celebrate the coming of the Holy Spirit on the early Christians long ago, and all the ways the Spirit is moving among us here and now.

Between these days of celebration are weeks of further formation so that your celebration, come Pentecost, may be full indeed. Easter Season is a time especially for helping the newly baptized with all the baptized grow in their understanding of Christian doctrine and to identify their gifts and callings for ministry in Christ's name. On Easter, both at the Great Vigil and again on Sunday morning, we exult in the resurrection of Jesus Christ from the dead. On Pentecost, we exult in what the Spirit is doing in the lives of those reborn or recommitted, and we bless and commission them for their ministries among us. And in the weeks between, in Sunday and in daily readings, we prepare ourselves to grow in our knowledge and love of God and to sharpen our own passions and skills for ministry in Christ's name and the Spirit's power.

Rev. Taylor Burton-Edwards

Resurrection of the Lord

Easter Day
Acts 10:34-43
Psalm 118:1-2, 14-24
1 Corinthians 15:19-26
Luke 24:1-12
or
John 20:1-18

Easter Evening
Isaiah 25:6-9
Psalm 114
1 Corinthians 5:6b-8
Luke 24:13-49

Reflection on Sunday
Daily: Psalm 118:1-2, 14-24

Monday
Joshua 10:16-27
1 Corinthians 5:6b-8

Tuesday
Judges 4:17-23; 5:24-31a
Revelation 12:1-12

Wednesday
2 Samuel 6:1-15
Luke 24:1-12

The General Rule of Discipleship
To witness to Jesus Christ in the world and to follow his teachings
through acts of compassion, justice, worship, and devotion under the guidance of the Holy Spirit.

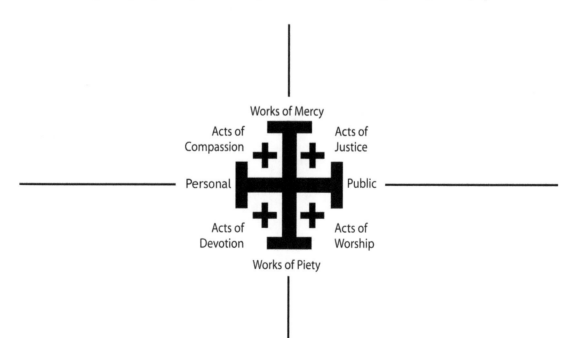

A Word from John Wesley

Who then are "the poor in spirit?" Without question, the humble; they who know themselves; who are convinced of sin; those to whom God hath given that first repentance, which is previous to faith in Christ. . . . He has a deep sense of the loathsome leprosy of sin, which he brought with him from his mother's womb, which overspreads his whole soul, and totally corrupts every power and faculty thereof.

Sermon 21: "Upon Our Lord's Sermon on the Mount 1," § I.4

A Hymn from Charles Wesley

Sinners, dismiss your fear,
The joyful tidings hear!
This the word that Jesus said,
O believe, and feel it true,
Christ is risen from the dead,
Lives the Lord who died for you!

Haste, to his tomb repair,
And see the tokens there;
See the place where Jesus lay,
Mark the burial-clothes he wore:
Angels near his relics stay,
Guards of him who dies no more.

Why then art thou cast down,
Thou poor afflicted one?
Full of doubts, and griefs, and fears,
Look into that open grave!
Died he not to dry thy tears?
Rose he not thy soul to save?

(*Hymns for Our Lord's Resurrection*—1746, #2:1-3)

Prayers, Comments & Questions

We exult in your love, O God of the living, for you made the tomb of death the womb from which you bring forth your Son, the firstborn of a new creation, and you anointed the universe with the fragrant Spirit of his resurrection. Make us joyful witnesses to this good news, that all humanity may one day gather at the feast of new life in the kingdom where you reign for ever and ever. Amen.

Second Sunday of Easter

Preparation for Sunday
Daily: Psalm 150

Thursday
1 Samuel 17:1-23
Acts 5:12-16

Friday
1 Samuel 17:19-32
Acts 5:17-26

Saturday
1 Samuel 17:32-51
Luke 24:36-40

Sunday
Acts 5:27-32
Psalm 118:14-29 *or*
Psalm 150
Revelation 1:4-8
John 20:19-31

Reflecting on Sunday
Daily: Psalm 122

Monday
Esther 7:1-10
Revelation 1:9-20

Tuesday
Esther 8:1-17
Revelation 2:8-11

Wednesday
Esther 9:1-5, 18-23
Luke 12:4-12

The General Rule of Discipleship
*To witness to Jesus Christ in the world and to follow his teachings
through acts of compassion, justice, worship, and devotion under the guidance of the Holy Spirit.*

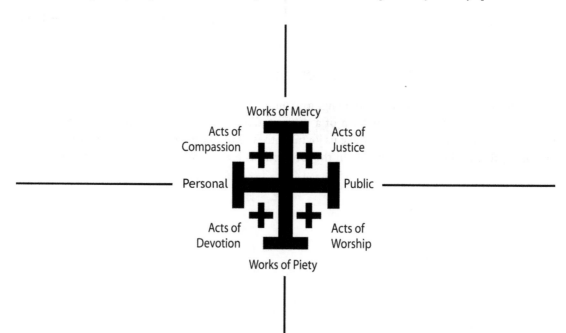

A Word from John Wesley

Our Lord has hitherto been more immediately employed in removing the hindrances of true religion: Such is pride, the first, grand hindrance of all religion, which is taken away by poverty of spirit; levity and thoughtlessness, which prevent any religion from taking root in the soul, till they are removed by holy mourning; such are anger, impatience, discontent, which are all healed by Christian meekness. And when once these hindrances are removed, these evil diseases of the soul, which were continually raising false cravings therein, and filling it with sickly appetites, the native appetite of a heaven-born spirit returns; it hungers and thirsts after righteousness: And "blessed are they which do hunger and thirst after righteousness; for they shall be filled."

Sermon 22: "Upon Our Lord's Sermon on the Mount 2," § II.1

A Hymn from Charles Wesley

Sinners, dismiss your fear,
The joyful tidings hear!
This the word that Jesus said,
O believe, and feel it true,
Christ is risen from the dead,
Lives the Lord who died for you!

Why then art thou cast down,
Thou poor afflicted one?
Full of doubts, and griefs, and fears,
Look into that open grave!
Died he not to dry thy tears?
Rose he not thy soul to save?

To purge thy guilty stain
He died, and rose again:
Wherefore dost thou weep and mourn?
Sinner, lift thine heart and eye,
Turn thee, to thy Jesus turn,
See thy loving Savior nigh.

(*Hymns for our Lord's Resurrection*—1746, #2:1, 3, & 5)

Prayers, Comments & Questions

O God, you raised up Jesus Christ as your faithful witness and the firstborn of the dead. By your Holy Spirit, help us to witness to him, so that those who have not yet seen may come to believe in him who is, and was, and is to come. Amen.

Third Sunday of Easter

Preparation for Sunday
Daily: Psalm 30

Thursday
Isaiah 5:11-17
Revelation 3:14-22

Friday
Isaiah 6:1-4
Revelation 4:1-11

Saturday
Genesis 18:1-8
Luke 14:12-14

Sunday
Acts 9:1-20
Psalm 30
Revelation 5:11-14
John 21:1-19

Reflection on Sunday
Daily: Psalm 121

Monday
Ezekiel 1:1-25
Acts 9:19b-31

Tuesday
Ezekiel 1:26—2:1
Acts 26:1-18

Wednesday
Isaiah 6:1-8
Luke 5:1-11

The General Rule of Discipleship
To witness to Jesus Christ in the world and to follow his teachings
through acts of compassion, justice, worship, and devotion under the guidance of the Holy Spirit.

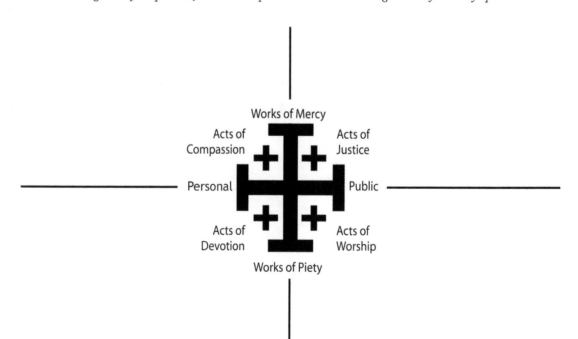

A Word from John Wesley

How excellent things are spoken of the love of our neighbour! It is "the fulfilling of the law," "the end of the commandment." Without this, all we have, all we do, all we suffer, is of no value in the sight of God. But it is that love of our neighbour which springs from the love of God: Otherwise itself is nothing worth. It behoves us, therefore, to examine well upon what foundation our love of our neighbour stands; whether it is really built upon the love of God; whether we do "love him because he first loved us;" whether we are pure in heart: For this is the foundation which shall never be moved. "Blessed are the pure in heart: For they shall see God."

Sermon 23: "Upon Our Lord's Sermon on the Mount-3," § I.1

A Hymn from Charles Wesley

All ye that seek the Lord who died,
Your God for sinners crucified,
Prevent the earliest dawn, and come
To worship at his sacred tomb.

Bring the sweet spices of your sighs,
Your contrite hearts, and streaming eyes,
Your sad complaints, and humble fears;
Come, and embalm him with your tears.

While thus ye love your souls t'employ,
Your sorrow shall be turned to joy:
Now, now let all your grief be oe'er
Believe, and ye shall weep no more.

Haste then, ye souls that first believe,
Who dare the gospel-word receive,
Your faith with joyful hearts confess,
Be bold, be Jesus' witnesses.

Go tell the followers of your Lord
Their Jesus is to life restored;
He lives, that they his life may find;
He lives, to quicken all mankind.

(*Hymns for our Lord's Resurrection*—1746, #1:1-3, 11-12)

Prayers, Comments & Questions

God of victory over death, your Son revealed himself again and again, and convinced his followers of his glorious resurrection. Grant that we may know his risen presence, in love obediently feed his sheep, and care for the lambs of his flock, until we join the hosts of heaven in worshiping you and praising him who is worthy of blessing and honor, glory and power, for ever and ever. Amen.

Fourth Sunday of Easter

Preparation for Sunday
Daily: Psalm 23

Thursday
Ezekiel 11:1-25
Revelation 5:1-10

Friday
Ezekiel 20:39-44
Revelation 6:1—7:4

Saturday
Ezekiel 28:25-26
Luke 12:29-32

Sunday
Acts 9:36-43
Psalm 23
Revelation 7:9-17
John 10:22-30

Reflection on Sunday
Daily: Psalm 100

Monday
Ezekiel 37:15-28
Revelation 15:1-4

Tuesday
Ezekiel 45:1-9
Acts 9:32-35

Wednesday
Jeremiah 50:17-20
John 10:31-42

The General Rule of Discipleship
*To witness to Jesus Christ in the world and to follow his teachings
through acts of compassion, justice, worship, and devotion under the guidance of the Holy Spirit.*

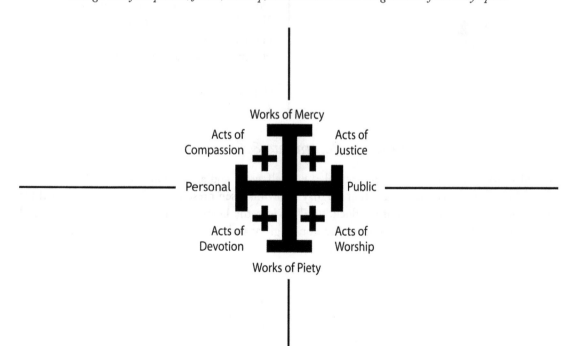

A Word from John Wesley

Indeed were we wholly to separate ourselves from sinners, how could we possibly answer that character which our Lord gives us in these very words? "Ye" (Christians, ye that are lowly, serious and meek; ye that hunger after righteousness, that love God and man, that do good to all, and therefore suffer evil; ye) "are the salt of the earth:" It is your very nature to season whatever is round about you. It is the nature of the divine savour which is in you, to spread to whatsoever you touch; to diffuse itself, on every side, to all those among whom you are.

Sermon 24: "Upon Our Lord's Sermon on the Mount 4," § I.7

A Hymn from Charles Wesley

Who can now presume to fear?
Who despair his Lord to see?
Jesus, wilt thou not appear,
Show thyself alive to me?
Yes, my God, I dare not doubt,
Thou shalt all my sins remove;
Thou hast cast a legion out,
Thou wilt perfect me in Love.

Surely thou hast called me now!
Now I hear the voice divine,
At thy wounded feet I bow,
Wounded for whose sins but mine!
I have nailed him to the tree,
I have sent him to the grave:
But the Lord is risen for me,
Hold of him by faith I have.

Hear, ye brethren of the Lord,
(Such he you vouchsafes to call)
O believe the gospel-word,
Christ hath died, and rose for all:
Turn ye from your sins to God,
Haste to Galilee, and see
Him, who bought thee with his blood,
Him, who rose to live in thee.

(*Hymns for our Lord's Resurrection*—
1746, #3:4-5, 7)

Prayers, Comments & Questions

God of comfort and compassion, through Jesus, your Son, you lead us to the water of life and the table of your bounty. May we who have received the tender love of our Good Shepherd be strengthened by your grace to care for your flock. Amen.

Fifth Sunday of Easter

Preparation for Sunday
Daily: Psalm 148

Thursday
Ezekiel 2:8—3:11
Revelation 10:1-11

Friday
Daniel 7:13-14
Revelation 11:15

Saturday
Daniel 7:27
Revelation 11:16-19

Sunday
Acts 11:1-18
Psalm 148
Revelation 21:1-6
John 13:31-35

Reflection on Sunday
Daily: Psalm 133

Monday
1 Samuel 20:1-23, 35-42
Acts 11:19-26

Tuesday
2 Samuel 1:4-27
Acts 11:27-30

Wednesday
Leviticus 19:9-18
Luke 10:25-28

The General Rule of Discipleship
To witness to Jesus Christ in the world and to follow his teachings
through acts of compassion, justice, worship, and devotion under the guidance of the Holy Spirit.

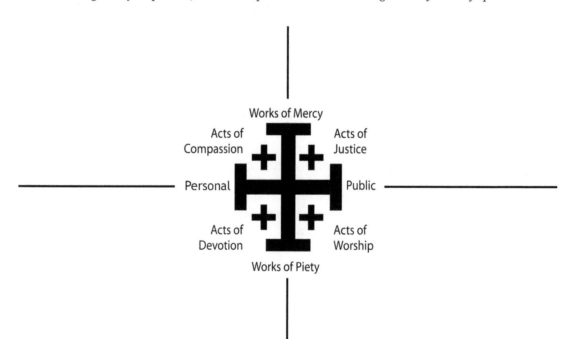

A Word from John Wesley

It is impossible, indeed, to have too high an esteem for "the faith of God's elect." And we must all declare, "By grace ye are saved through faith; not of works, lest any man should boast." We must cry aloud to every penitent sinner, "Believe in the Lord Jesus Christ, and thou shalt be saved." But, at the same time, we must take care to let all men know, we esteem no faith but that which worketh by love [Gal. 5:6]; and that we are not saved by faith, unless so far as we are delivered from the power as well as the guilt of sin.

Sermon 25: "Upon Our Lord's Sermon on the Mount 5," § III.9

A Hymn from Charles Wesley

Jesus, the rising Lord of all,
His Love to man commends,
Poor worms he blushes not to call
His brethren and his friends.

Who basely all forsook their Lord
In his distress, and fled,
To these he sends the joyful word,
When risen from the dead.

Sinners, I rose again to show
Your sins are all forgiven,
And mount above the skies, that you
May follow me to heaven.

(*Hymns for our Lord's Resurrection*—1746–1781, 4:1-2, 6)

Prayers, Comments & Questions

Alpha and Omega, First and Last, glory outshining all the lights of heaven: Pour out upon us your Spirit of faithful love and abundant compassion, so that we may rejoice in the splendor of your works while we wait in expectation for the new heaven and the new earth you promise when Christ shall come again. Amen.

Sixth Sunday of Easter

Preparation for Sunday
Daily: Psalm 67

Thursday
Proverbs 2:1-5
Acts 15:36-41

Friday
Proverbs 2:6-8
Acts 16:1-8

Saturday
Proverbs 2:9-15
Luke 19:1-10

Sunday
Acts 16:9-15
Psalm 67
Revelation 21:10, 22—22:5
John 14:23-29 *or*
John 5:1-9

Reflection on Sunday
Daily: Psalm 93

Monday
1 Chronicles 12:16-22
Revelation 21:5-14

Tuesday
2 Chronicles 15:1-15
Revelation 21:15-22

Wednesday
2 Chronicles 34:20-33
Luke 2:25-38

The General Rule of Discipleship
To witness to Jesus Christ in the world and to follow his teachings
through acts of compassion, justice, worship, and devotion under the guidance of the Holy Spirit.

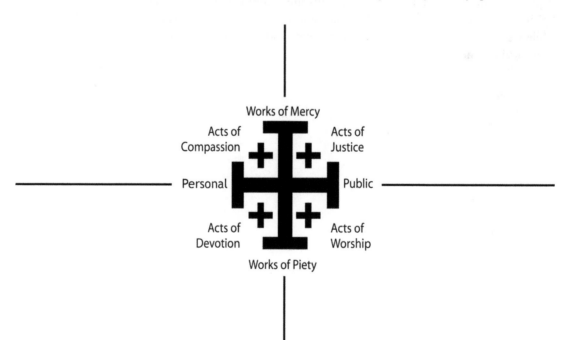

A Word from John Wesley

From works of charity or mercy our Lord proceeds to those which are termed works of piety. "And when thou prayest," saith he, "thou shalt not be as the hypocrites are; for they love to pray standing in the synagogues, and in the corners of the streets, that they may be seen of men."—"Thou shalt not be as the hypocrites are." Hypocrisy, then, or insincerity, is the first thing we are to guard against in prayer. Beware not to speak what thou dost not mean. Prayer is the lifting up of the heart to God: All words of prayer, without this, are mere hypocrisy.

Sermon 26: "Upon Our Lord's Sermon on the Mount 6," § II.1

A Hymn from Charles Wesley

Object of all our knowledge here,
Our one desire, and hope below,
Jesus, the crucified, draw near,
And with thy sad disciples go:
Our thoughts and words to thee are known,
We commune of thyself alone.

How can it be, our reason cries,
That God should leave his throne above?
Is it for man the Immortal dies!
For man, who tramples on his love!
For man, who nailed him to the tree!
O love! O God! He dies for me!

Ah! Lord, if thou indeed art ours,
If thou for us hast burst the tomb,
Visit us with thy quickening powers,
Come to thy mournful followers come,
Thyself to thy weak members join,
And fill us with the life divine.

(*Hymns for our Lord's Resurrection*—1746, #5:1-2, 5)

Prayers, Comments & Questions

Gracious God, through a vision you sent forth Paul to preach the gospel and called the women to the place of prayer on the sabbath. Grant that we may be sent like Paul and be found like Lydia, our hearts responsive to your word and open to go where you lead us. Amen.

Seventh Sunday of Easter

Preparation for Sunday
Daily: Psalm 97

Thursday
Ascension of the Lord
Acts 1:1-11
Psalm 47 or 93
Ephesians 1:15-23
Luke 24:44-53

Friday
Exodus 33:12-17
Revelation 22:6-9

Saturday
Exodus 33:18-23
John 1:14-18

Sunday
Acts 16:16-34
Psalm 97
Revelation 22:12-14,
16-17, 20-21
John 17:20-26

Reflection on Sunday
Daily: Psalm 29

Monday
Exodus 40:16-38
Acts 16:35-40

Tuesday
2 Chronicles 5:2-14
Acts 26:19-29

Wednesday
Ezekiel 3:12-21
Luke 9:18-27

The General Rule of Discipleship
*To witness to Jesus Christ in the world and to follow his teachings
through acts of compassion, justice, worship, and devotion under the guidance of the Holy Spirit.*

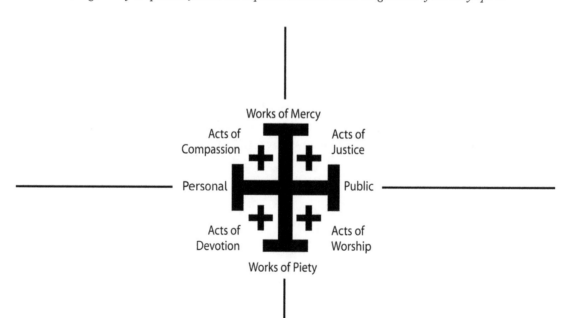

A Word from John Wesley

A Fifth and more weighty reason for fasting is, that it is an help to prayer; particularly when we set apart larger portions of time for private prayer. . . . And it is chiefly, as it is an help to prayer, that it has so frequently been found a means, in the hand of God, of confirming and increasing, not one virtue, not chastity only, . . . but also seriousness of spirit, earnestness, sensibility and tenderness of conscience, deadness to the world, and consequently the love of God, and every holy and heavenly affection.

Sermon 27: "Upon Our Lord's Sermon on the Mount 7," § II.6

A Hymn from Charles Wesley

Come in, with thy disciples sit,
Nor suffer us to ask in vain,
Nourish us, Lord, with living meat.
Our souls with heavenly bread sustain;
Break to us now the mystic bread,
And bid us on thy body feed.

Honor the means ordained by thee,
The great unbloody sacrifice,
The deep tremendous mystery;
Thyself in our enlightened eyes
Now in the broken bread make known,
And shew us thou art all our own.

(*Hymns for our Lord's Resurrection*—1746, #6:5-6)

Prayers, Comments & Questions

Ascension of the Lord

Precious Love, your ascended Son promised the gift of holy power. Send your Spirit of revelation and wisdom, that in the blessed freedom of hope, we may witness to the grace of forgiveness and sing songs of joy with the peoples of earth to the One who makes us one body. Amen.

Seventh Sunday of Easter

God of boundless grace, you call us to drink freely of the well of life and to share the love of your holy being. May the glory of your love, made known in the victory of Jesus Christ, our Savior, transform our lives and the world he lived and died to save. We ask this in his name and for his sake. Amen.

Day of Pentecost

Preparation for Sunday
Daily: Psalm 104:24-34, 35b

Thursday
Isaiah 32:11-17
Galatians 5:16-25

Friday
Isaiah 44:1-4
Galatians 6:7-10

Saturday
2 Kings 2:1-15a
Luke 1:5-17

Sunday
Acts 2:1-21 *or*
Genesis 11:1-9
Psalm 104:24-34, 35b
Romans 8:14-17 *or*
Acts 2:1-21
John 14:8-17, 25-27

Reflection on Sunday
Daily: Psalm 48

Monday
Joel 2:18-29
1 Corinthians 2:1-11

Tuesday
Ezekiel 11:14-25
1 Corinthians 2:12-16

Wednesday
Numbers 24:1-14
Luke 1:26-38

The General Rule of Discipleship
To witness to Jesus Christ in the world and to follow his teachings
through acts of compassion, justice, worship, and devotion under the guidance of the Holy Spirit.

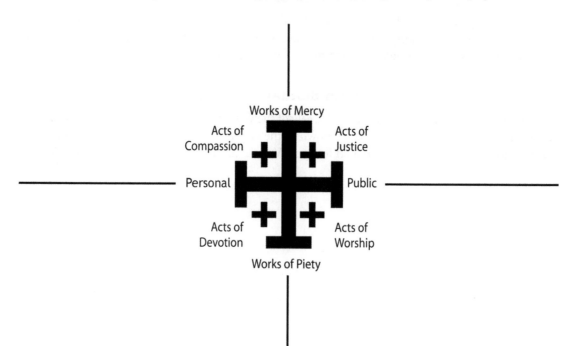

A Word from John Wesley

Give to the poor with a single eye, with an upright heart, and write, "So much given to God." For "Inasmuch as ye did it unto one of the least of these my brethren, ye have done it unto me."

This is the part of a "faithful and wise steward": Not to sell either his houses or lands, or principal stock, be it more or less, unless some peculiar circumstance should require it; and not to desire or endeavour to increase it, any more than to squander it away in vanity; but to employ it wholly to those wise and reasonable purposes for which his Lord has lodged it in his hands.

Sermon 28: "Upon Our Lord's Sermon on the Mount 8," ¶ 26

A Hymn from Charles Wesley

Father of everlasting grace,
Thy goodness and thy truth we praise,
Thy goodness and thy truth we prove:
Thou hast in honor of thy Son
The gift unspeakable sent down
The Spirit of life, and power, and love.

Thou hast the prophecy fulfilled,
The grand original compact sealed,
For which thy word and oath were joined:
The promise to our fallen head
To every child of Adam made,
Is now poured out on all mankind.

The purchased Comforter is given,
For Jesus is returned to heaven,
To claim, and then the grace impart:
Our day of Pentecost is come,
And God vouchsafes to fix his home
In every poor expecting heart.

(*Hymns for Whitsunday*—1746, #1:1-3)

Prayers, Comments & Questions

Living God, you have created all that is. Send forth your Spirit to renew and restore us, that we may proclaim your good news in ways and words that all will understand and believe. Amen.

Season After Pentecost

Disciples in Ministry in Christ's Name and the Spirit's Power

This season is sometimes also referred to as "Ordinary Time," but it is intended to be far from "ordinary" in terms of its purposes in supporting and strengthening your discipleship to Jesus Christ. The word "Ordinary" here actually refers only to the "ordinal numbers" (first, second, third, and so on) used to refer to which Sunday after Pentecost a given Sunday may be throughout this season.

Rather than ordinary or "ho-hum," the idea of this season is to support disciples and the whole congregation in living out the gifts and callings discerned during Easter Season and commissioned on the Day of Pentecost. In the Northern Hemisphere, this season typically corresponds with "summer," when schools are out and wide varieties of vacation schedules may mean the ability to coordinate or even operate some ministries in the congregation (such as Sunday school or some choirs) may be challenged or curtailed until a relaunch in the fall. This scheduling situation makes it even more critical for congregations and individuals to make sure the profound formational and missional purposes of this season are not overlooked but intentionally planned for.

If you are using *A Disciple's Journal*, chances are you are already intent on strengthening your own discipleship. Let me encourage you to take another step. Ask your pastor to work with you to gather others who will take these months as an intentional journey of accountable discipleship and growth in ministry with you. Your congregation may not be able to provide a "program" for everyone who does this, but your pastor can certainly help you gather a "coalition of the willing" who will.

As you do, keep in mind that with the exceptions of Trinity Sunday and Christ the King Sunday, which begin and end this season, and All Saints, which falls during it, the three major tracks of readings (Old Testament, Epistle, and Gospel) are all "semi-continuous" during this season. None is intended to relate to the other, except for the "Bookend Sundays" and All Saints. The Old Testament readings are selections from the stories of the prophets, kings, and patriarchs/matriarchs (depending on the year). The Epistle readings explore the meaning and practice of the Christian life in particular early Christian communities. And the Gospel readings take us on a journey through the ministry and teaching of Jesus.

As suggested for the Season after Epiphany, you may wish to coordinate the way you and your group focus your energy and attention on the daily readings through these months with the particular stream of texts your congregation's worship leaders focus on during this time, as a means to help reinforce the themes of the Sunday readings with your daily discipleship and ministry throughout these months.

Rev. Taylor Burton-Edwards

Trinity Sunday

Preparation for Sunday
Daily: Psalm 8

Thursday
Proverbs 3:13-18
Ephesians 1:17-19

Friday
Proverbs 3:19-26
Ephesians 4:1-6

Saturday
Proverbs 4:1-9
Luke 2:41-52

Sunday
Proverbs 8:1-4, 22-31
Psalm 8
Romans 5:1-5
John 16:12-15

Reflection on Sunday
Daily: Psalm 124

Monday
Proverbs 7:1-4
Ephesians 4:7-16

Tuesday
Proverbs 8:4-21
Ephesians 5:15-20

Wednesday
Daniel 1:1-21
Luke 1:46b-55

The General Rule of Discipleship
*To witness to Jesus Christ in the world and to follow his teachings
through acts of compassion, justice, worship, and devotion under the guidance of the Holy Spirit.*

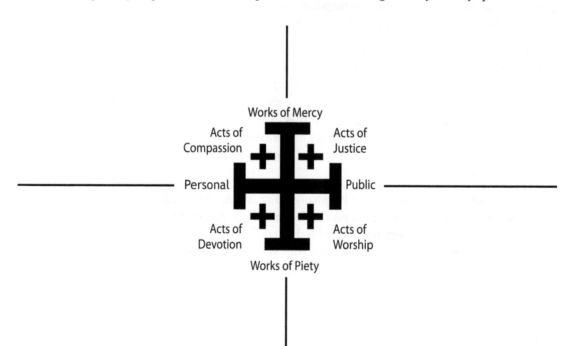

A Word from John Wesley

Now to love God in the manner the Scripture describes, in the manner God himself requires of us, and by requiring engages to work in us,—is to love him as the ONE GOD; that is, "with all our heart, and with all our soul, and with all our mind, and with all our strength;"—it is to desire God alone for his own sake; and nothing else, but with reference to him;—to rejoice in God;—to delight in the Lord; not only to seek, but find, happiness in him; to enjoy God as the chiefest among ten thousand; to rest in him, as our God and our all;—in a word, to have such a possession of God as makes us always happy.

Sermon 29: "Upon Our Lord's Sermon on the Mount 9," ¶ 5

A Hymn from Charles Wesley

A wonderful plurality
In the true God by faith we see,
Who hear the record of the Son
"I and my Father are but one;"
In different Persons we proclaim
On God eternally the same.

Father and Son in nature join,
Each Person is alike divine:
Alike by heaven and earth adored,
Thy Spirit makes the glorious third:
Co-equal, co-eternal Three,
Show thyself One, great God, in me.

(*Hymns on the Trinity*—1767, #18)

Prayers, Comments & Questions

God of heaven and earth, before the foundation of the universe and the beginning of time you are the triune God: the Author of creation, the eternal Word of salvation, and the life-giving Spirit of wisdom. Guide us to all truth by your Spirit, that we may proclaim all that Christ revealed and rejoice in the glory he shared with us. Glory and praise to you, Father, Son, and Holy Spirit, now and forever. Amen.

Sunday between May 24 and 28 inclusive
(if after Trinity Sunday)

Preparation for Sunday
Daily: Psalm 92:1-4, 12-15

Thursday
Proverbs 13:1-12
Romans 5:12—6:2

Friday
Proverbs 15:1-9
1 Thessalonians 4:13-18

Saturday
Isaiah 30:8-17
John 16:1-4a

Sunday
Isaiah 55:10-13
Psalm 92:1-4, 12-15
1 Corinthians 15:51-58
Luke 6:39-49

Reflection on Sunday
Daily: Psalm 1

Monday
Jeremiah 24:1-10
1 Corinthians 16:1-12

Tuesday
Jeremiah 29:10-19
1 Corinthians 16:13-24

Wednesday
Proverbs 5:1-23
Luke 14:34-35

The General Rule of Discipleship
*To witness to Jesus Christ in the world and to follow his teachings
through acts of compassion, justice, worship, and devotion under the guidance of the Holy Spirit.*

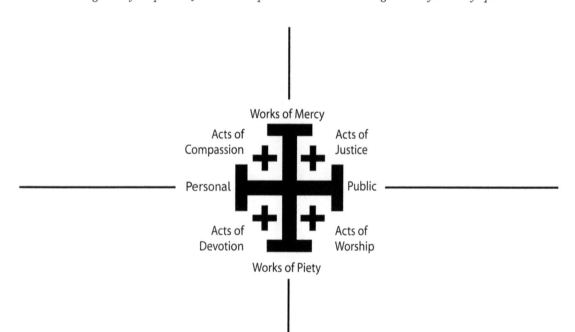

A Word from John Wesley

One thing more we are to understand by serving God, and that is, the obeying him; the glorifying him with our bodies, as well as with our spirits; the keeping his outward commandments; the zealously doing whatever he hath enjoined; the carefully avoiding whatever he hath forbidden; the performing all the ordinary actions of life with a single eye and a pure heart, offering them all in holy, fervent love, as sacrifices to God through Jesus Christ.

Sermon 29: "Upon Our Lord's Sermon on the Mount 9," ¶ 7

A Hymn from Charles Wesley

Eternal Spirit, come
Into thy meanest home,
From thine high and Holy Place
Where thou dost in Glory reign,
Stoop in condescending grace,
Stoop to the poor heart of man.

For thee our hearts we lift
And wait the heavenly gift:
Giver, Lord of life divine,
To our dying souls appear,
Grant the grace for which we pine,
Give thyself the Comforter.

No gift or comfort we
Would have distinct from thee,
Spirit, principle of grace,
Sum of our desires thou art,
Fill us with thy holiness,
Breathe thyself into our heart.

(*Hymns for Whitsunday*—1746, 3:1-3)

Prayers, Comments & Questions

Holy, holy, holy God, in calling forth creation from the void, revealing yourself in human flesh, and pouring forth your wisdom to guide us, you manifest your concern for your whole universe. You invite us, as your people, to gather the world's needs into our hearts and bring them before you. Amen.

Sunday between May 29 and June 4 inclusive
(if after Trinity Sunday)

Preparation for Sunday
Daily: Psalm 96

Thursday
1 Kings 12:20-33
2 Corinthians 5:11-17

Friday
1 Kings 16:29-34
2 Corinthians 11:1-6

Saturday
1 Kings 18:1-19
Luke 4:31-37

Sunday
1 Kings 18:20-39
Psalm 96
Galatians 1:1-12
Luke 7:1-10

Reflection on Sunday
Daily: Psalm 135

Monday
Ezekiel 8:1-18
Acts 8:26-40

Tuesday
Ezekiel 14:1-11
Acts 3:1-10

Wednesday
Ezekiel 14:12-23
Mark 7:24-30

The General Rule of Discipleship
*To witness to Jesus Christ in the world and to follow his teachings
through acts of compassion, justice, worship, and devotion under the guidance of the Holy Spirit.*

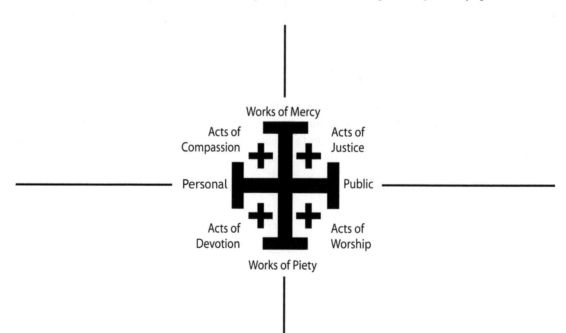

A Word from John Wesley

To serve mammon is, Lastly, to obey the world, by outwardly conforming to its maxims and customs; to walk as other men walk, in the common road, in the broad, smooth, beaten path; to be in the fashion; to follow a multitude; to do like the rest of our neighbours; that is, to do the will of the flesh and the mind, to gratify our appetites and inclinations; to sacrifice to ourselves; aim at our own ease and pleasure, in the general course both of our words and actions. Now what can be more undeniably clear than that we cannot thus serve God and mammon?

Sermon 29: "Upon Our Lord's Sermon on the Mount 9," ¶ 11

A Hymn from Charles Wesley

Sinners, lift up your hearts,
The Promise to receive!
Jesus himself imparts,
He comes in man to live;
The Holy Ghost to man is given;
Rejoice in God sent down from heaven.

Jesus is glorified,
And gives the Comforter,
His Spirit to reside
In all his members here:
The Holy Ghost to man is given;
Rejoice in God sent down from heaven.

To make an end of sin,
And Satan's works destroy,
He brings his kingdom in,
Peace, righteousness, and joy,
The Holy Ghost to man is given;
Rejoice in God sent down from heaven.

Hymns for Whitsunday—1746, 4:1-3

Prayers, Comments & Questions

O God, living Lord, you are the author of faith. Engrave on our hearts the gospel revealed in Jesus Christ and brought near to us by your Holy Spirit, that we may attest to this faith in lives that are pleasing to you. Amen.

Sunday between June 5 and 11 inclusive
(if after Trinity Sunday)

Preparation for Sunday
Daily: Psalm 146

Thursday
Exodus 29:1-9
Acts 22:6-21

Friday
Numbers 15:17-26
Acts 26:1-11

Saturday
Joshua 9:1-27
Matthew 9:2-8

Sunday
1 Kings 17:8-24
Psalm 146
Galatians 1:11-24
Luke 7:11-17

Reflection on Sunday
Daily: Psalm 68:1-10, 19-20

Monday
Job 22:1-20
Galatians 2:1-10

Tuesday
Job 24:9-25
Galatians 2:11-14

Wednesday
Job 31:16-23
Luke 8:40-56

The General Rule of Discipleship
*To witness to Jesus Christ in the world and to follow his teachings
through acts of compassion, justice, worship, and devotion under the guidance of the Holy Spirit.*

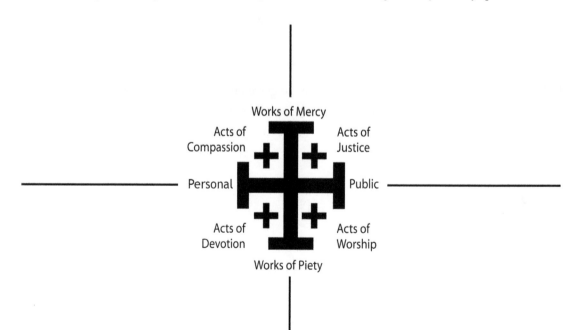

Works of Mercy

Acts of Compassion — Acts of Justice

Personal — Public

Acts of Devotion — Acts of Worship

Works of Piety

A Word from John Wesley

Does not every reasonable, every thinking man see that he cannot possibly serve God and mammon? Because there is the most absolute contrariety, the most irreconcilable enmity between them. The contrariety between the most opposite things on earth, between fire and water, darkness and light, vanishes into nothing when compared to the contrariety between God and mammon. So that, in whatsoever respect you serve the one, you necessarily renounce the other. Do you believe in God through Christ? Do you trust in him as your strength, your help, your shield, and your exceeding great reward? As your happiness? Your end in all, above all things? Then you cannot trust in riches.

Sermon 29: "Upon Our Lord's Sermon on the Mount 9," ¶ 14

A Hymn from Charles Wesley

Father, admit our lawful claim,
Let us that ask receive:
To us that ask in Jesus' name
Thou shalt thy Spirit give.

Jesus hath spoke the faithful word
On them that ask him here,
Thou shalt, in honour of our Lord,
The Holy Ghost confer.

If evil we, by nature know
To give our children food,
Much more thou wilt on us bestow
The soul-sustaining good.

Our holy heavenly Father thou
Regard'st thy children's prayer:
Answer, and send, O send us now
The promised Comforter.

We seek, thou know'st we seek thy face;
Let us the blessing find:
Open the door of faith and grace
To us, and all mankind.

Hymns for Whitsunday—1746, 5:1-5

Prayers, Comments & Questions

Provident God, whose love enfolds the helpless, the needy, and those who mourn, give us strength through Jesus Christ to be instruments of your compassion to those who are desolate or wounded by life. Amen.

Sunday between June 12 and 18 inclusive
(if after Trinity Sunday)

Preparation for Sunday
Daily: Psalm 5:1-8

Thursday
1 Kings 20:1-22
James 4:1-7

Friday
1 Kings 20:23-34
Romans 11:1-10

Saturday
1 Kings 20:35-43
Luke 5:17-26

Sunday
1 Kings 21:1-21a
Psalm 5:1-8
Galatians 2:15-21
Luke 7:36—8:3

Reflection on Sunday
Daily: Psalm 83

Monday
Genesis 31:17-35
Galatians 3:1-9

Tuesday
2 Samuel 19:31-43
Galatians 3:10-14

Wednesday
Malachi 3:5-12
Mark 2:1-12

The General Rule of Discipleship
To witness to Jesus Christ in the world and to follow his teachings
through acts of compassion, justice, worship, and devotion under the guidance of the Holy Spirit.

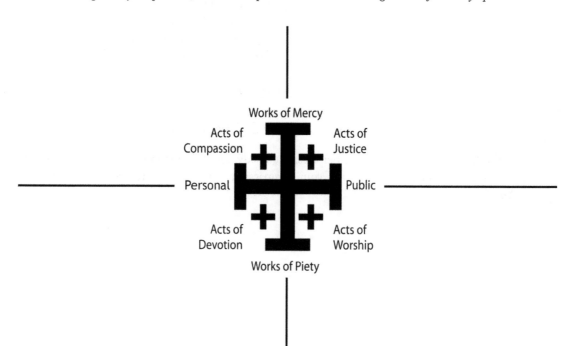

A Word from John Wesley

Our Lord does not here require, that we should be utterly without thought, even touching the concerns of this life. A giddy, careless temper is at the farthest remove from the whole religion of Jesus Christ. Neither does he require us to be "slothful in business," to be slack and dilatory therein. This, likewise, is contrary to the whole spirit and genius of his religion. A Christian abhors sloth as much as drunkenness; and flees from idleness as he does from adultery. He well knows, that there is one kind of thought and care with which God is well pleased; which is absolutely needful for the due performance of those outward works unto which the providence of God has called him.

Sermon 29: "Upon Our Lord's Sermon on the Mount 9," ¶ 16

A Hymn from Charles Wesley

Spirit of holiness, and root,
Thy gracious God-delighting fruit
Is joy, fidelity and peace,
Meekness which no affront can move,
Truth, temperance, long-suffering, love,
And universal righteousness.

Restorer of the sin-sick mind,
Our souls a perfect soundness find
Thro' all their powers in thee renewed,
Spirit of life and might divine,
By thee we in the image shine,
In all the strength and life of God.

Thou dost the living power exert
T'invig'rate and confirm the heart
Of those who feel thy work begun
To exercise our every grace,
Quicken us in the glorious race,
'Till all the glorious race is run.

(*Hymns for Whitsunday*—1746, 31:1-3)

Prayers, Comments & Questions

God of compassion, you suffer in the grief of your people, and you are present to heal and forgive. May the sun of your justice rise on every night of oppression, and may the warm rays of your healing love renew each troubled mind; for you are the God of salvation and new life, made known to us in Jesus Christ our Lord. Amen.

Sunday between June 19 and 25 inclusive
(if after Trinity Sunday)

Preparation for Sunday
Daily: Psalm 42 & 43

Thursday
Genesis 24:1-21
Romans 2:17-29

Friday
Job 6:14-30
Galatians 3:15-22

Saturday
Proverbs 11:3-13
Matthew 9:27-34

Sunday
1 Kings 19:1-15a
Psalm 42 & 43
Galatians 3:23-29
Luke 8:26-39

Reflection on Sunday
Daily: Psalm 59

Monday
2 Kings 9:1-13
1 Corinthians 1:18-31

Tuesday
2 Kings 9:14-26
Ephesians 2:11-22

Wednesday
2 Kings 9:30-37
Luke 9:37-43a

The General Rule of Discipleship
To witness to Jesus Christ in the world and to follow his teachings
through acts of compassion, justice, worship, and devotion under the guidance of the Holy Spirit.

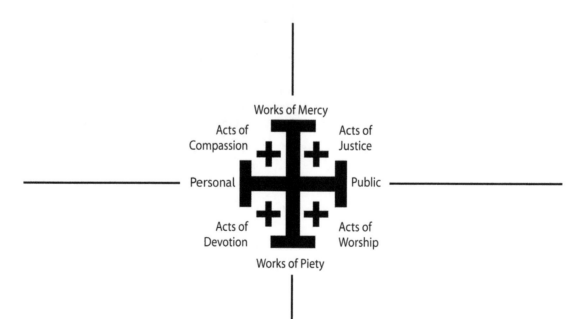

A Word from John Wesley

But that your prayer may have its full weight with God, see that ye be in charity with all men; for otherwise it is more likely to bring a curse than a blessing on your own head; nor can you expect to receive any blessing from God while you have not charity towards your neighbour. Therefore, let this hindrance be removed without delay. Confirm your love towards one another, and towards all men. And love them, not in word only, but in deed and in truth. "Therefore, all things whatsoever ye would that men should do to you, do ye even so to them; for this is the law and the prophets."

Sermon 30: "Upon Our Lord's Sermon on the Mount 10," ¶ 21

A Hymn from Charles Wesley

Come, ye that love the Lord,
And let your joys be known;
Join in a song with sweet accord
While ye surround his throne.
Let those refuse to sing
Who never knew our God,
But servants of the heavenly king
May speak their joys abroad.

The God that rules on high,
That all the earth surveys,
That rides upon the stormy sky,
And calms the roaring seas;
This awful God is ours,
Our father and our love;
He will send down his heavenly powers
To carry us above.

(*Collection—1781*, 12:1-2)

Prayers, Comments & Questions

God our refuge and hope, when race, status, or gender divide us, when despondency and despair haunt and afflict us, when community lies shattered: comfort and convict us with the stillness of your presence, that we may confess all you have done, through Christ to whom we belong and in whom we are one. Amen.

Sunday between June 26 and July 2 inclusive

Preparation for Sunday
Daily: Psalm 77:1-2, 11-20

Thursday
1 Kings 22:29-40, 51-53
2 Corinthians 13:5-10

Friday
2 Kings 1:1-12
Galatians 4:8-20

Saturday
2 Kings 1:13-18; 2:3-5
Luke 9:21-27

Sunday
2 Kings 2:1-2, 6-14
Psalm 77:1-2, 11-20
Galatians 5:1, 13-25
Luke 9:51-62

Reflection on Sunday
Daily: Psalm 75

Monday
2 Kings 2:15-22
1 John 2:7-11

Tuesday
2 Kings 3:4-20
Ephesians 5:6-20

Wednesday
2 Kings 4:1-7
Matthew 10:16-25

The General Rule of Discipleship
To witness to Jesus Christ in the world and to follow his teachings
through acts of compassion, justice, worship, and devotion under the guidance of the Holy Spirit.

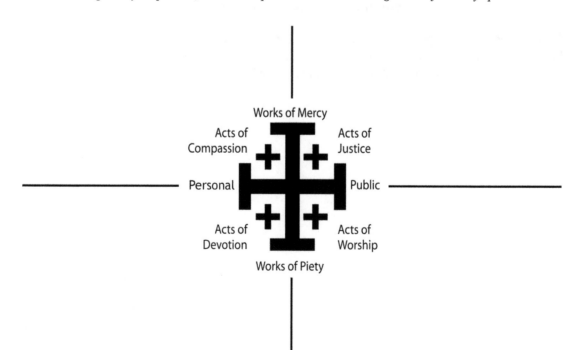

A Word from John Wesley

For, "narrow is the way that leadeth unto life;" the way of universal holiness. Narrow indeed is the way of poverty of spirit; the way of holy mourning; the way of meekness; and that of hungering and thirsting after righteousness. Narrow is the way of mercifulness; of love unfeigned; the way of purity of heart; of doing good unto all men; and of gladly suffering evil, all manner of evil, for righteousness' sake.

Sermon 31: "Upon Our Lord's Sermon on the Mount 11," § II.3

A Hymn from Charles Wesley

Happy the souls to Jesus joined,
And saved by grace alone;
Walking in all his ways, they find
Their heaven on earth begun.

The church triumphant in thy love,
Their mighty joys we know;
They sing the Lamb in hymns above:
And we in hymns below.

Thee in thy glorious realm they praise,
And bow before thy throne!
We in the kingdom of thy grace:
The kingdoms are but one.

The holy to the holiest leads;
From thence our spirits rise,
And he that in thy statutes treads
Shall meet thee in the skies.

(*Collection*—1781, #15)

Prayers, Comments & Questions

O God, you set us free in Jesus Christ with a power greater than all that would keep us captive. Grant that we might live gracefully in our freedom without selfishness or arrogance, and through love become slaves to the freedom of the gospel for the sake of your reign. Amen.

Sunday between July 3 and 9 inclusive

Preparation for Sunday
Daily: Psalm 30

Thursday
2 Kings 4:8-17
Romans 7:14-25

Friday
2 Kings 4:18-31
2 Corinthians 8:1-7

Saturday
2 Kings 4:32-37
Luke 9:1-6

Sunday
2 Kings 5:1-14
Psalm 30
Galatians 6:1-16
Luke 10:1-11, 16-20

Reflection on Sunday
Daily: Psalm 6

Monday
2 Kings 5:15-19a
Acts 19:21-27

Tuesday
2 Kings 5:19b-27
Acts 19:28-41

Wednesday
2 Kings 6:1-7
Luke 10:13-16

The General Rule of Discipleship
To witness to Jesus Christ in the world and to follow his teachings
through acts of compassion, justice, worship, and devotion under the guidance of the Holy Spirit.

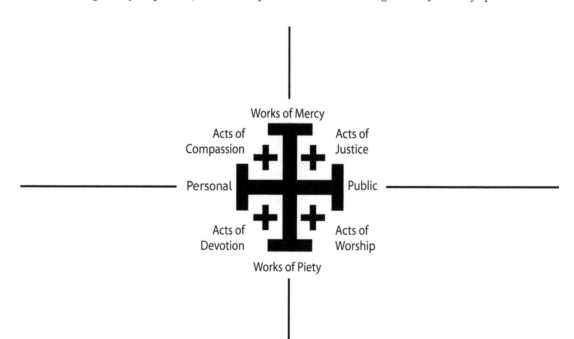

A Word from John Wesley

Then humble yourselves before him. Cry unto him out of the dust, that he may first quicken thy soul; give thee the faith that worketh by love; that is lowly and meek, pure and merciful, zealous of good works, rejoicing in tribulation, in reproach, in distress, in persecution for righteousness' sake! So shall "the Spirit of glory and of Christ rest upon thee," and it shall appear that God hath sent thee. So shalt thou indeed "do the work of an Evangelist, and make full proof of thy ministry." So shall the word of God in thy mouth be "an hammer that breaketh the rocks in pieces!" It shall then be known by thy fruits that thou art a Prophet of the Lord, even by the children whom God hath given thee.

Sermon 32: "Upon Our Lord's Sermon on the Mount 12," § III.14

A Hymn from Charles Wesley

The gates of hell cannot prevail,
The church on earth can never fail.
Ah, join me to thy secret ones!
Ah, gather all thy living stones!

Scattered o'er all the earth they lie,
Till thou collect them with thine eye!
Draw by the music of thy name,
And charm into a beauteous frame.

For this the pleading Spirit groans,
And cries in all thy banished ones:
Greatest of gifts, thy love impart,
And make us of one mind and heart.

Join every soul that looks to thee
In bonds of perfect charity:
Now, Lord, the glorious fullness give,
And all in all forever live.

(*Collection—1781*, #16:8-11)

Prayers, Comments & Questions

God of fresh beginnings, you make all things new in the wisdom of Jesus Christ. Make us agents of your transforming power and heralds of your reign of justice and peace, that all may share in the healing Christ brings. Amen.

Sunday between July 10 and 16 inclusive

Preparation for Sunday
Daily: Psalm 82

Thursday
Amos 1:1—2:3
James 2:14-26

Friday
Amos 2:4-11
Acts 7:9-16

Saturday
Amos 2:12—3:8
John 3:16-21

Sunday
Amos 7:7-17
Psalm 82
Colossians 1:1-14
Luke 10:25-37

Reflection on Sunday
Daily: Psalm 7

Monday
Amos 3:9—4:5
James 2:1-7

Tuesday
Amos 4:6-13
1 John 3:11-17

Wednesday
Amos 5:1-9
Matthew 25:31-46

The General Rule of Discipleship
To witness to Jesus Christ in the world and to follow his teachings
through acts of compassion, justice, worship, and devotion under the guidance of the Holy Spirit.

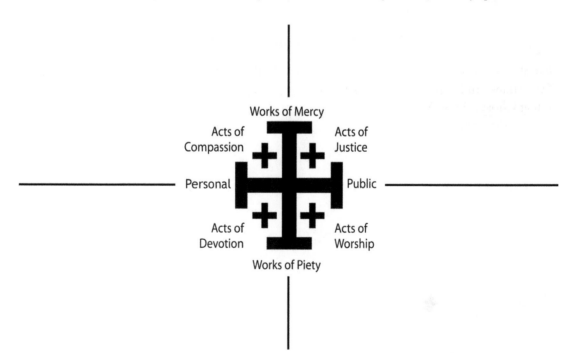

A Word from John Wesley

Now, seeing thou canst do all things through Christ strengthening thee, be merciful as thy Father in heaven is merciful! Love thy neighbour as thyself! Love friends and enemies as thy own soul! And let thy love be longsuffering and patient towards all men. Let it be kind, soft, benign; inspiring thee with the most amiable sweetness, and the most fervent and tender affection. Let it rejoice in the truth, wheresoever it is found; the truth that is after godliness.

Sermon 33: "Upon Our Lord's Sermon on the Mount 13," § III.10

A Hymn from Charles Wesley

Rejoice evermore
With angels above,
In Jesus's power,
In Jesus's love;
With glad exultation
Your triumph proclaim,
Ascribing salvation
To God and the Lamb.

Thou, Lord, our relief
In trouble hast been,
Hast saved us from grief,
Hast saved us from sin;
The power of thy Spirit
Hath set our hearts free;
And now we inherit
All fullness in thee.

(*Collection*—1781, #19:1-2)

Prayers, Comments & Questions

Divine Judge, you framed the earth with love and mercy and declared it good; yet we, desiring to justify ourselves, judge others harshly, without knowledge or understanding. Keep us faithful in prayer, that we may be filled with the knowledge of your will and not ignore or pass by another's need but plumb the depths of love in showing mercy. Amen.

Sunday between July 17 and 23 inclusive

Preparation for Sunday
Daily: Psalm 52

Thursday
Amos 5:10-17
Hebrews 5:1-6

Friday
Amos 5:18-27
Ephesians 3:14-21

Saturday
Amos 6:1-14
Luke 8:4-10

Sunday
Amos 8:1-12
Psalm 52
Colossians 1:15-28
Luke 10:38-42

Reflection on Sunday
Daily: Psalm 119:17-32

Monday
Amos 7:1-6
Colossians 1:27—2:7

Tuesday
Amos 8:13—9:4
1 John 2:1-6

Wednesday
Amos 9:5-15
John 6:41-51

The General Rule of Discipleship
*To witness to Jesus Christ in the world and to follow his teachings
through acts of compassion, justice, worship, and devotion under the guidance of the Holy Spirit.*

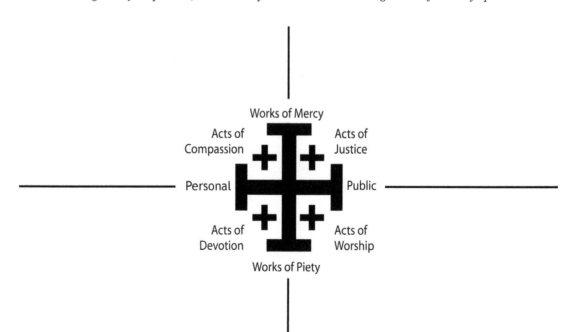

A Word from John Wesley

And if thou are thoroughly convinced that [the law] is the offspring of God, that it is the copy of all his inimitable perfections, and that it is "holy, and just, and good," but especially to them that believe; then, instead of casting it away as a polluted thing, see that thou cleave to it more and more. Never let the law of mercy and truth, of love to God and man, of lowliness, meekness, and purity, forsake thee. . . . Keep close to the law, if thou wilt keep close to Christ; hold it fast; let it not go.

Sermon 34: "The Original, Nature, Property, and Use of the Law," § IV.9

A Hymn from Charles Wesley

Weary souls that wander wide
From the central point of bliss,
Turn to Jesus crucified,
Fly to those dear wounds of his:
Sink into the purple flood;
Rise into the life of God!

Find in Christ the way of peace,
Peace unspeakable, unknown;
By his pain he gives you ease,
Life by his expiring groan;
Rise exalted by his fall,
Find in Christ your all in all.

(*Collection*—1781, #20:1-2)

Prayers, Comments & Questions

Ever-faithful God, whose being is perfect righteousness: Reconcile us in your Son with the helpless and the needy, with those we would ignore or oppress, and with those we have called enemies, that we may serve all people as your hands of love and sit at the feet of those who need our compassionate care. Amen.

Sunday between July 24 and 30 inclusive

Preparation for Sunday
Daily: Psalm 85

Thursday
Hosea 4:1-19
Acts 1:15-20

Friday
Hosea 5:1-15
Acts 2:22-36

Saturday
Hosea 1:11—2:15
Luke 8:22-25

Sunday
Hosea 1:2-10
Psalm 85
Colossians 2:6-19
Luke 11:1-13

Reflection on Sunday
Daily: Psalm 44

Monday
Hosea 2:14—3:5
Colossians 2:16—3:1

Tuesday
Hosea 6:1-10
Romans 9:30—10:4

Wednesday
Hosea 6:11—7:16
Matthew 5:43-48

The General Rule of Discipleship
*To witness to Jesus Christ in the world and to follow his teachings
through acts of compassion, justice, worship, and devotion under the guidance of the Holy Spirit.*

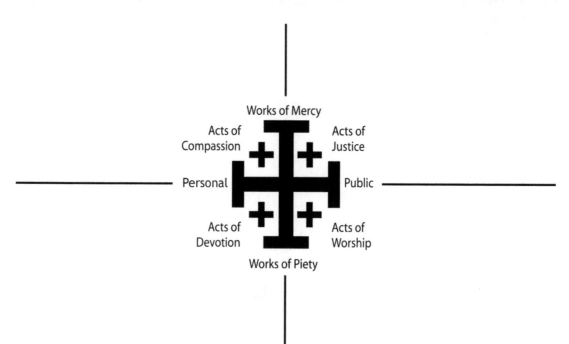

A Word from John Wesley

But the truth lies between both. We are, doubtless, justified by faith. This is the cornerstone of the whole Christian building. We are justified without the works of the law, as any previous condition of justification; but they are an immediate fruit of that faith whereby we are justified. So that if good works do not follow our faith, even all inward and outward holiness, it is plain our faith is nothing worth; we are yet in our sins. Therefore, that we are justified by faith, even by our faith without works, is no ground for making void the law through faith; or for imagining that faith is a dispensation from any kind or degree of holiness.

Sermon 35: "The Law Established Through Faith 1," § II.6

A Hymn from Charles Wesley

O believe the record true,
God to you his Son hath given!
Ye may now be happy too,
Find on earth the life of heaven;
Live the life of heaven above,
All the life of glorious love.

This the universal bliss,
Bliss for every soul designed;
God's original promise this,
God's great gift to all mankind:
Blest in Christ this moment be!
Blest to all eternity!

(*Collection*—1781, #20:3-4)

Prayers, Comments & Questions

Living God, you raise us to fullness of being in sharing the Christ-life together. Teach us to pray and grant us hopeful persistence in seeking your will and your way, that by the power of the Spirit, love and faithfulness may meet to disarm the powers of the world. Amen.

Sunday between July 31 and August 6 inclusive

Preparation for Sunday
Daily: Psalm 107:1-9, 43

Thursday
Hosea 8:1-14
Romans 11:33-36

Friday
Hosea 9:1-17
Ephesians 4:17-24

Saturday
Hosea 10:1-15
Mark 10:17-22

Sunday
Hosea 11:1-11
Psalm 107:1-9, 43
Colossians 3:1-11
Luke 12:13-21

Reflection on Sunday
Daily: Psalm 60

Monday
Hosea 11:12—12:14
Colossians 3:18—4:1

Tuesday
Hosea 13:1-16
Colossians 4:2-6

Wednesday
Hosea 14:1-9
Luke 12:22-31

The General Rule of Discipleship
*To witness to Jesus Christ in the world and to follow his teachings
through acts of compassion, justice, worship, and devotion under the guidance of the Holy Spirit.*

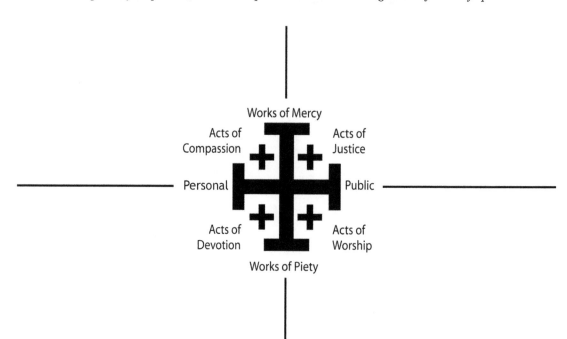

A Word from John Wesley

But still we should not preach Christ, according to his word, if we were wholly to confine ourselves to this: We are not ourselves clear before God, unless we proclaim him in all his offices. To preach Christ, as a workman that needeth not to be ashamed, is to preach him, not only as our great High Priest, . . .—but likewise as the Prophet of the Lord, . . .—yea, and as remaining a King for ever; as giving laws to all whom he has bought with his blood; as restoring those to the image of God, whom he had first re-instated in his favour; as reigning in all believing hearts until he has "subdued all things to himself,"—until he hath utterly cast out all sin, and brought in everlasting righteousness.

Sermon 36: "The Law Established Through Faith 2," § I.6

A Hymn from Charles Wesley

Behold, the Saviour of mankind
Nailed to the shameful tree;
How vast the love that him inclined
To bleed and die for thee!

Hark, how he groans, while nature shakes,
And earth's strong pillars bend!
The temple's veil in sunder breaks,
The solid marbles rend.

'Tis done! The precious ransom's paid.
"Receive my soul," he cries!
See where he bows his sacred head!
He bows his head and dies.

But soon he'll break death's envious chain,
And in full glory shine.
O Lamb of God, was ever pain,
Was ever love like thine!

(*Collection*—1781, #22)

Prayers, Comments & Questions

Generous God, in abundance you give us things both spiritual and physical. Help us to hold lightly the fading things of this earth and grasp tightly the lasting things of your kingdom, so that what we are and do and say may be our gifts to you through Christ, who beckons all to seek the things above, where he lives and reigns with you and the Holy Spirit. Amen.

Sunday between August 7 and 13 inclusive

Preparation for Sunday
Daily: Psalm 50:1-8, 22-23

Thursday
Isaiah 9:8-17
Romans 9:1-9

Friday
Isaiah 9:18—10:4
Acts 7:1-8

Saturday
Isaiah 1:2-9, 21-23
Matthew 6:19-24

Sunday
Isaiah 1:1, 10-20
Psalm 50:1-8, 22-23
Hebrews 11:1-3, 8-16
Luke 12:32-40

Reflection on Sunday
Daily: Psalm 11

Monday
Isaiah 2:1-4
Hebrews 11:1-7

Tuesday
Isaiah 24:1-13
Hebrews 11:17-28

Wednesday
Isaiah 24:14-23
Luke 12:41-48

The General Rule of Discipleship
To witness to Jesus Christ in the world and to follow his teachings
through acts of compassion, justice, worship, and devotion under the guidance of the Holy Spirit.

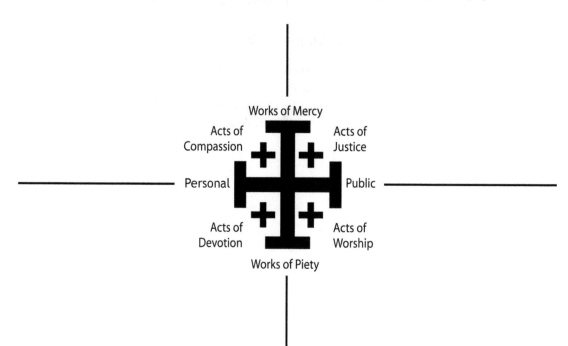

A Word from John Wesley

Beware, lastly, of imagining you shall obtain the end without using the means conducive to it. God can give the end without any means at all; but you have no reason to think He will. Therefore constantly and carefully use all those means which He has appointed to be the ordinary channels of His grace. Use every means which either reason or Scripture recommends, as conducive (through the free love of God in Christ) either to the obtaining or increasing any of the gifts of God.

Sermon 37: "The Nature of Enthusiasm," ¶ 39

A Hymn from Charles Wesley

Extended on a cursed tree,
Besmeared with dust, and sweat, and blood,
See there, the King of glory see!
Sinks and expires the Son of God.

Who, who, my Saviour, this hath done?
Who could thy sacred body wound?
No guilt thy spotless heart hath known,
No guile hath in thy lips been found.

I, I alone have done the deed!
'Tis I thy sacred flesh have torn,
My sins have caused thee, Lord, to bleed,
Pointed the nail, and fixed the thorn.

(*Collection*—1781, #23:1-3)

Prayers, Comments & Questions

God of judgment and grace, you ask not for sacrifices but lives of trusting faith that acknowledge your power and mercy. Give us faith as deep and strong as Abraham's and Sarah's, that we may follow you through all our days as did Jesus Christ our Savior. Amen.

Sunday between August 14 and 20 inclusive

Preparation for Sunday
Daily: Psalm 80:1-2, 8-19

Thursday
Isaiah 2:5-11
Hebrews 10:26-31

Friday
Isaiah 3:1-17
Hebrews 10:32-39

Saturday
Isaiah 3:18—4:6
Matthew 24:15-27

Sunday
Isaiah 5:1-7
Psalm 80:1-2, 8-19
Hebrews 11:29—12:2
Luke 12:49-56

Reflection on Sunday
Daily: Psalm 74

Monday
Isaiah 5:8-23
1 John 4:1-6

Tuesday
Isaiah 5:24-30
Acts 7:44-53

Wednesday
Isaiah 27:1-13
Luke 19:45-48

The General Rule of Discipleship
To witness to Jesus Christ in the world and to follow his teachings
through acts of compassion, justice, worship, and devotion under the guidance of the Holy Spirit.

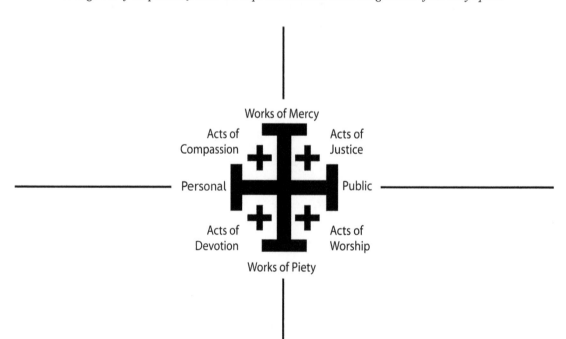

A Word from John Wesley

Yea, if you would observe our Lord's direction in its full meaning and extent, then remember his word: "He that is not for us is against us; and he that gathereth not with me scattereth": he that gathereth not men into the kingdom of God, assuredly scatters them from it. For there can be no neuter in this war. Every one is either on God's side, or on Satan's. Are you on God's side? Then you will not only not forbid any man that casts out devils, but you will labour, to the uttermost of your power, to forward him in the work. You will readily acknowledge the work of God and confess the greatness of it.

Sermon 38: "A Caution Against Bigotry," § III.12

A Hymn from Charles Wesley

The burden for me to sustain
Too great, on thee, my Lord, was laid;
To heal me, thou hast borne my pain,
To bless me, thou a curse wast made.

In the devouring lion's teeth,
Torn, and forsook of all I lay;
Thou sprang'st into the jaws of death,
From death to save the helpless prey.

My Saviour, how shall I proclaim?
How pay the mighty debt I owe?
Let all I have, and all I am,
Ceaseless to all thy glory show.

(*Collection*—1781, #23:4-6)

Prayers, Comments & Questions

Judge eternal, you love justice and hate oppression; you give peace to those who seek it, and you condemn the rage of violence. Give us courage to take our stand with all victims of bloodshed and greed and, following your servants and prophets, look to Jesus, the pioneer and perfecter of our faith. Amen.

Sunday between August 21 and 27 inclusive

Preparation for Sunday
Daily: Psalm 71:1-6

Thursday
Jeremiah 6:1-19
Hebrews 12:3-17

Friday
Jeremiah 6:20-30
Acts 17:1-9

Saturday
Jeremiah 1:1-3, 11-19
Luke 6:1-5

Sunday
Jeremiah 1:4-10
Psalm 71:1-6
Hebrews 12:18-29
Luke 13:10-17

Reflection on Sunday
Daily: Psalm 10

Monday
Jeremiah 7:1-15
Hebrews 3:7—4:11

Tuesday
Jeremiah 7:16-26
Revelation 3:7-13

Wednesday
Jeremiah 7:27-34
Luke 6:6-11

The General Rule of Discipleship
To witness to Jesus Christ in the world and to follow his teachings
through acts of compassion, justice, worship, and devotion under the guidance of the Holy Spirit.

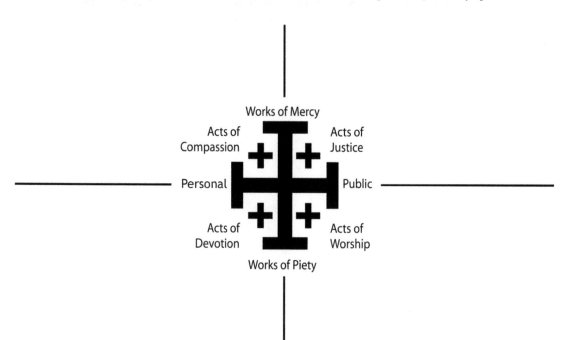

Works of Mercy

Acts of Compassion

Acts of Justice

Personal

Public

Acts of Devotion

Acts of Worship

Works of Piety

A Word from John Wesley

Dost thou believe in the Lord Jesus Christ, "God over all, blessed for ever?" Is he revealed in thy soul? Dost thou know Jesus Christ and him crucified? Does he dwell in thee, and thou in him? Is he formed in thy heart by faith? Having absolutely disclaimed all thy own works, thy own righteousness, hast thou "submitted thyself unto the righteousness of God, which is by faith in Christ Jesus?" Art thou "found in him, not having thy own righteousness, but the righteousness which is by faith?" And art thou, through him, "fighting the good fight of faith, and laying hold of eternal life?"

Sermon 39: "Catholic Spirit," § I.13

A Hymn from Charles Wesley

Too much to thee I cannot give,
Too much I cannot do for thee;
Let all thy love, and all thy grief,
Grav'n on my heart for ever be!

The meek, the still, the lowly mind
O may I learn from thee my God;
And love, with softest pity joined,
For those that trample on thy blood.

Still let thy tears, thy groans, thy sighs,
O'erflow my eyes, and heave my breast,
Till loose from flesh and earth I rise,
And ever in thy bosom rest.

(*Collection*—1781, #23:7-9)

Prayers, Comments & Questions

Living God, you formed us in the womb and appointed us to be prophets to the nations. Stretch out your hand to cure our infirmity and dispel our fear, that we may know the freedom of serving you in Christ and proclaim the wonders you have done. Amen.

Sunday between August 28 and September 3 inclusive

Preparation for Sunday
Daily: Psalm 81:1, 10-16

Thursday
Jeremiah 11:1-17
1 Peter 3:8-12

Friday
Jeremiah 12:1-13
1 Peter 4:7-11

Saturday
Jeremiah 2:1-3, 14-22
Matthew 20:20-28

Sunday
Jeremiah 2:4-13
Psalm 81:1, 10-16
Hebrews 13:1-8, 15-16
Luke 14:1, 7-14

Reflection on Sunday
Daily: Psalm 58

Monday
Jeremiah 2:23-37
Hebrews 13:7-21

Tuesday
Jeremiah 3:1-14
Titus 1:1-9

Wednesday
Jeremiah 3:15-25
Luke 14:15-24

The General Rule of Discipleship
To witness to Jesus Christ in the world and to follow his teachings
through acts of compassion, justice, worship, and devotion under the guidance of the Holy Spirit.

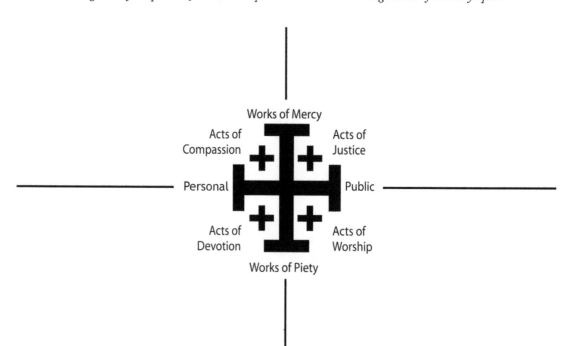

A Word from John Wesley

Now the Word of God plainly declares, that even those who are justified, who are born again in the lowest sense, "do not continue in sin;" that they cannot "live any longer therein;" (Rom. 6:1, 2) that they are "planted together in the likeness of the death" of Christ; (Rom. 6:5) that their "old man is crucified with him," the body of sin being destroyed, so that henceforth they do not serve sin; that being dead with Christ, they are free from sin; (Rom. 6:6, 7) that they are "dead unto sin, and alive unto God;" (Rom. 6:11) that "sin hath no more dominion over them," who are "not under the law, but under grace;" but that these, "being free from sin, are become the servants of righteousness." (Rom. 6:14, 18)

Sermon 40: "Christian Perfection," § II.3

A Hymn from Charles Wesley

Jesus, thou all-redeeming Lord,
Thy blessing we implore;
Open the door to preach thy word,
The great effectual door.

Gather the outcasts in and save
From sin and Satan's power,
And let them now acceptance have,
And know their gracious hour.

Lover of souls, thou know'st to prize
What thou hast bought so dear;
Come then, and in thy people's eyes
With all thy wounds appear!

(*Collection*—1781, #34:1-3)

Prayers, Comments & Questions

God of majestic glory, in humility you have revealed yourself in the incarnation of your Son, Jesus Christ, who took the lowest place among us that we might be raised to the heights of divinity. Teach us to walk the path he prepared for us, so that we might take a place at the table with all who seek the joy of his kingdom. Amen.

Sunday between September 4 and 10 inclusive

Preparation for Sunday
Daily: Psalm 139:1-6, 13-18

Thursday
Jeremiah 15:10-21
Philippians 2:25-30

Friday
Jeremiah 16:14—17:4
Colossians 4:7-17

Saturday
Jeremiah 17:14-27
Matthew 10:34-42

Sunday
Jeremiah 18:1-11
Psalm 139:1-6, 13-18
Philemon 1-21
Luke 14:25-33

Reflection on Sunday
Daily: Psalm 2

Monday
Jeremiah 18:12-23
1 Timothy 3:14—4:5

Tuesday
Jeremiah 19:1-15
1 Timothy 4:6-16

Wednesday
Jeremiah 20:1-18
Luke 18:18-30

The General Rule of Discipleship
To witness to Jesus Christ in the world and to follow his teachings
through acts of compassion, justice, worship, and devotion under the guidance of the Holy Spirit.

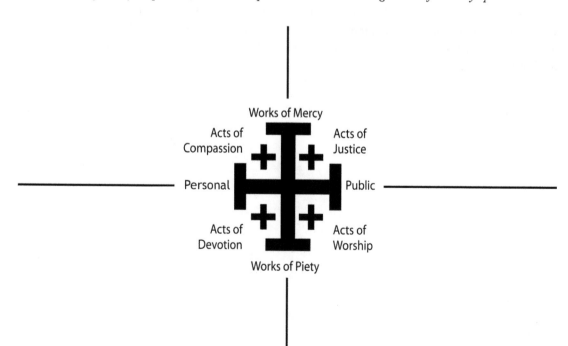

A Word from John Wesley

But many times we are not only "without God in the world," but also fighting against him; as there is in every man by nature a "carnal mind which is enmity against God:" No wonder, therefore, that men abound with unbelieving thoughts; either saying in their hearts, "There is no God," or questioning, if not denying, his power or wisdom, his mercy, or justice, or holiness. No wonder that they so often doubt of his providence, at least, of its extending to all events; or that, even though they allow it, they still entertain murmuring or repining thoughts. . . . Now by all these they make flat war with God: These are wandering thoughts of the highest kind.

Sermon 41: "Wandering Thoughts," § I.3

A Hymn from Charles Wesley

Jesus, the name high over all
In hell, or earth, or sky;
Angels and men before it fall,
And devils fear and fly.

Jesus, the name to sinners dear,
The name to sinners given!
It scatters all their guilty fear,
It turns their hell to heaven.

Jesus the prisoner's fetters breaks,
And bruises Satan's head,
Power into strengthless souls it speaks,
And life into the dead.

(*Collection*—1781, #36: 1-3)

Prayers, Comments & Questions

Creator God, you form us on the wheel of life as a potter molds the clay. Shape us into holy vessels, bearing the mark of your wise crafting, that we may remain strong and useful through years of faithful and obedient service in Christ's name. Amen.

Sunday between September 11 and 17 inclusive

Preparation for Sunday
Daily: Psalm 14

Thursday
Jeremiah 13:20-27
1 Timothy 1:1-11

Friday
Jeremiah 4:1-10
2 Peter 2:1-10a

Saturday
Jeremiah 4:13-21, 29-31
John 10:11-21

Sunday
Jeremiah 4:11-12, 22-28
Psalm 14
1 Timothy 1:12-17
Luke 15:1-10

Reflection on Sunday
Daily: Psalm 94

Monday
Jeremiah 5:1-17
1 Timothy 1:18-20

Tuesday
Jeremiah 5:18-31
2 Peter 3:8-13

Wednesday
Jeremiah 14:1-10, 17-22
Luke 22:31-33, 54-62

The General Rule of Discipleship
To witness to Jesus Christ in the world and to follow his teachings
through acts of compassion, justice, worship, and devotion under the guidance of the Holy Spirit.

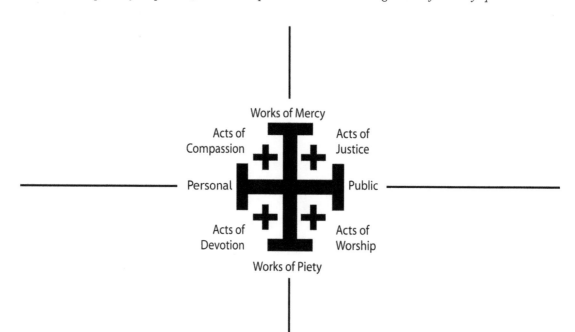

A Word from John Wesley

If in time past you have abused this blessed hope of being holy as he is holy, yet do not therefore cast it away. Let the abuse cease, the use remain. Use it now to the more abundant glory of God, and profit of your own soul. In steadfast faith, in calm tranquility of spirit, in full assurance of hope, rejoicing evermore for what God hath done, press ye on unto perfection! Daily growing in the knowledge of our Lord Jesus Christ, and going on from strength to strength, in resignation, in patience, in humble thankfulness for what ye have attained, and for what ye shall, run the race set before you, "looking unto Jesus," till, through perfect love, ye enter into his glory!

Sermon 42: "Satan's Devices," § II.8

A Hymn from Charles Wesley

O that the world might taste and see
The riches of his grace.
The arms of love that compass me
Would all mankind embrace.

O that my Jesu's heavenly charms
Might every bosom move!
Fly, sinners, fly into those arms
Of everlasting love.

His only righteousness I show,
His saving truth proclaim,
'Tis all my business here below,
To cry, "Behold the Lamb!"

Happy, if with my latest breath
I may but gasp his name!
Preach him to all, and cry in death,
"Behold! behold the Lamb."

(*Collection*—1781, #36:4-7)

Prayers, Comments & Questions

Merciful God, your desire to bring us into your commonwealth is so great that you seek us in the places of our ignorance and the forgotten corners where we hide in despair. Gather us into your loving embrace, and pour upon us your wise and holy Spirit, so that we may become faithful servants in whom you rejoice with all the company of heaven. Amen.

Sunday between September 18 and 24 inclusive

Preparation for Sunday
Daily: Psalm 79:1-9

Thursday
Jeremiah 12:14—13:11
Romans 3:1-8

Friday
Jeremiah 8:1-13
Romans 8:31-39

Saturday
Jeremiah 8:14-17; 9:2-11
Mark 12:41-44

Sunday
Jeremiah 8:18—9:1
Psalm 79:1-9
1 Timothy 2:1-7
Luke 16:1-13

Reflection on Sunday
Daily: Psalm 106:40-48

Monday
Jeremiah 9:12-26
Acts 4:1-12

Tuesday
Jeremiah 10:1-16
1 Corinthians 9:19-23

Wednesday
Jeremiah 10:17-25
Luke 20:45—21:4

The General Rule of Discipleship
To witness to Jesus Christ in the world and to follow his teachings
through acts of compassion, justice, worship, and devotion under the guidance of the Holy Spirit.

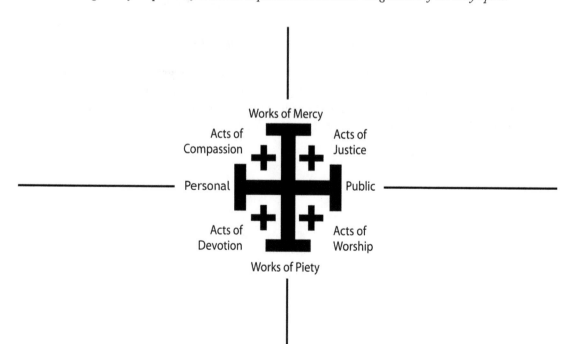

A Word from John Wesley

Taking the word in a more particular sense, faith is a divine evidence and conviction, not only that "God was in Christ, reconciling the world unto himself," but also that Christ loved me, and gave himself for me. It is by this faith (whether we term it the essence, or rather a property thereof) that we receive Christ; that we receive him in all his offices, as our Prophet, Priest, and King. It is by this that he is "made of God unto us wisdom, and righteousness, and sanctification, and redemption."

Sermon 43: "The Scripture Way of Salvation," § II.2

A Hymn from Charles Wesley

Summoned my labour to renew,
And glad to act my part,
Lord, in thy name my work I do,
And with a single heart.

End of my every action thou,
In all things thee I see;
Accept my hallowed labour now;
I do it unto thee.

Whate'er the Father views as thine
He views with gracious eyes;
Jesu, this mean oblation join
To thy great sacrifice.

Stamped with an infinite desert
My work he then shall own,
Well-pleased with me, when mine thou art,
And I his favourite son.

(*Collection*—1781, #320)

Prayers, Comments & Questions

When joy is gone and hearts are sick, O God, you give us Christ as our healing balm. He came in human flesh that he might give himself as a ransom for our salvation and anoint us with the Spirit of consolation and joy. Hear the cry of your people, that we may rejoice in the richness of your love and be faithful stewards of your many gifts. Amen.

Sunday between September 25 and October 1 inclusive

Preparation for Sunday
Daily: Psalm 91:1-6, 14-16

Thursday
Jeremiah 23:9-22
2 Corinthians 8:8-15

Friday
Jeremiah 23:23-32
Ephesians 2:1-10

Saturday
Jeremiah 24:1-10
Luke 9:43b-48

Sunday
Jeremiah 32:1-3a, 6-15
Psalm 91:1-6, 14-16
1 Timothy 6:6-19
Luke 16:19-31

Reflection on Sunday
Daily: Psalm 119:49-56

Monday
Jeremiah 32:16-35
Revelation 3:14-22

Tuesday
Jeremiah 32:36-44
James 5:1-6

Wednesday
Jeremiah 33:1-13
Matthew 19:16-22

The General Rule of Discipleship
To witness to Jesus Christ in the world and to follow his teachings
through acts of compassion, justice, worship, and devotion under the guidance of the Holy Spirit.

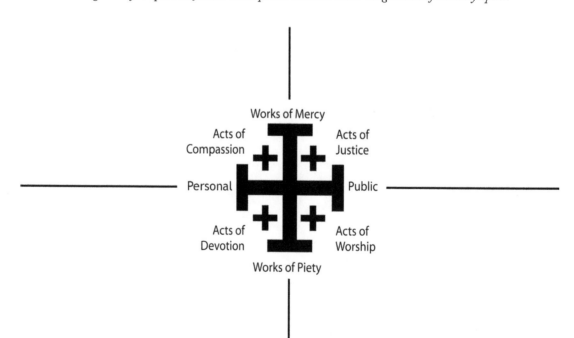

A Word from John Wesley

We may learn from hence, in the Third place, what is the proper nature of religion, of the religion of Jesus Christ. It is . . . God's method of healing a soul which is thus diseased. Hereby the great Physician of souls applies medicines to heal this sickness; to restore human nature, totally corrupted in all its faculties. God heals all our Atheism by the knowledge of Himself, and of Jesus Christ whom he hath sent; by giving us faith, a divine evidence and conviction of God, and of the things of God,—in particular, of this important truth, "Christ loved me"—and gave himself for me."

Sermon 44: "Original Sin," § III.3

A Hymn from Charles Wesley

Servant of all, to toil for man
Thou didst not, Lord, refuse;
Thy majesty did not disdain
To be employed for us!

Thy bright example I pursue,
To thee in all things rise;
And all I think, or speak, or do,
Is one great sacrifice.

Careless through outward cares I go,
From all distraction free;
My hands are but engaged below,
My heart is still with thee.

(*Collection*—1781, #321)

Prayers, Comments & Questions

God Eternal, you inspired Jeremiah to buy a piece of land when no one could see a future in it. Grant us such commitment to the future of your people, that you will always have workers for your vineyard and harvesters for your fields. Amen.

Sunday between October 2 and 8 inclusive

Preparation for Sunday
Daily: Lam. 3:19-26

Thursday
Jeremiah 52:1-11
Revelation 2:8-11

Friday
Jeremiah 52:12-30
Revelation 2:12-29

Saturday
Lamentations 1:7-15
Matthew 20:29-34

Sunday
Lamentations 1:1-6
Lamentations 3:19-26
or Psalm 137
2 Timothy 1:1-14
Luke 17:5-10

Reflection on Sunday
Daily: Psalm 137

Monday
Lamentations 1:16-22
James 1:2-11

Tuesday
Lamentations 2:13-22
1 John 5:1-5, 13-21

Wednesday
Lamentations 5:1-22
Mark 11:12-14, 20-24

The General Rule of Discipleship
To witness to Jesus Christ in the world and to follow his teachings
through acts of compassion, justice, worship, and devotion under the guidance of the Holy Spirit.

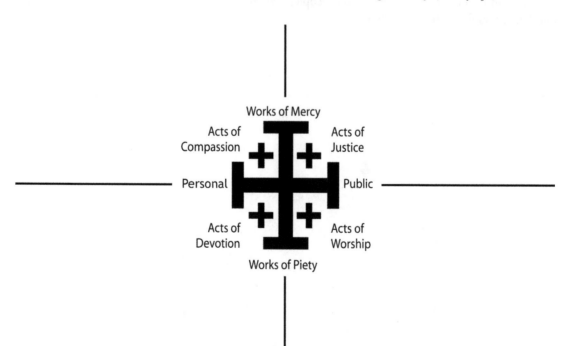

A Word from John Wesley

. . . to what end, is it necessary that we should be born again? It is very easily discerned, that this is necessary, First, in order to holiness. . . . Gospel holiness is no less than the image of God stamped upon the heart; it is no other than the whole mind which was in Christ Jesus; it consists of all heavenly affections and tempers mingled together in one. . . . Now, this holiness can have no existence till we are renewed in the image of our mind. It cannot commence in the soul till . . . we are born again; which, therefore, is absolutely necessary in order to holiness.

Sermon 45: "The New Birth," § III.1

A Hymn from Charles Wesley

God of almighty love,
By whose sufficient grace
I lift my heart to things above,
And humbly seek thy face;
Through Jesus Christ the just
My faint desires receive,
And let me in thy goodness trust,
And to thy glory live.

Spirit of faith, inspire
My consecrated heart;
Fill me with pure, celestial fire,
With all thou hast and art;
My feeble mind transform,
And perfectly renewed,
Into a saint exalt a worm;
A worm exalt to God!

(*Collection*—1781, #322: 1, 3)

Prayers, Comments & Questions

God, the refuge of wanderers and exiles, the mother and father of the homeless, you weep with those who are uprooted from their homeland, and you suffer with those who exist without shelter and security. Grant that your faithful love may reach out, and that your healing mercy rise like the dawn on all who are oppressed. We ask this through Jesus, your Son, who knew hardship and died outside the city wall. Amen.

Sunday between October 9 and 15 inclusive

Preparation for Sunday
Daily: Psalm 66:1-12

Thursday
Jeremiah 25:1-14
2 Timothy 1:13-18

Friday
Jeremiah 27:1-22
2 Timothy 2:1-7

Saturday
Jeremiah 28:1-17
Luke 5:12-16

Sunday
Jeremiah 29:1, 4-7
Psalm 66:1-12
2 Timothy 2:8-15
Luke 17:11-19

Reflection on Sunday
Daily: Psalm 102:1-17

Monday
Jeremiah 29:8-23
Acts 26:24-29

Tuesday
Jeremiah 29:24-32
Ephesians 6:10-20

Wednesday
Jeremiah 25:15-32
Matthew 10:5-15

The General Rule of Discipleship
*To witness to Jesus Christ in the world and to follow his teachings
through acts of compassion, justice, worship, and devotion under the guidance of the Holy Spirit.*

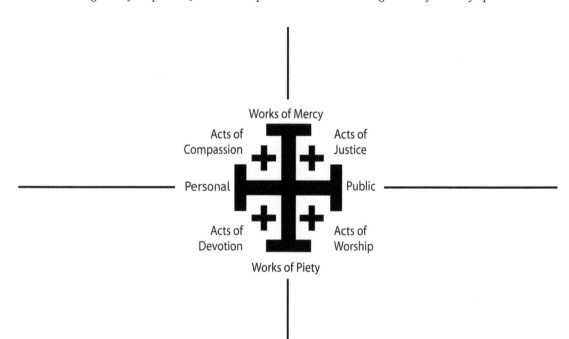

A Word from John Wesley

O stir yourself up before the Lord! Arise, and shake yourself from the dust; wrestle with God for the mighty blessing; pour out your soul unto God in prayer, and continue therein with all perseverance! Watch! Awake out of sleep; and keep awake! Otherwise there is nothing to be expected, but that you will be alienated more and more from the light and life of God.

Sermon 46: "The Wilderness State," § III.5

A Hymn from Charles Wesley

Forth in thy name, O Lord, I go,
My daily labour to pursue,
Thee, only thee resolved to know,
In all I think, or speak, or do.

The task thy wisdom has assigned
O let me cheerfully fulfill,
In all my works thy presence find,
And prove thy acceptable will.

Thee may I set at my right hand
Whose eyes my inmost substance see,
And labour on at thy command,
And offer all my works to thee.

(*Collection*—1781, #323:1-3)

Prayers, Comments & Questions

In your love, O God of hosts, your people find healing. Grant that the pains of our journey may not obscure the presence of Christ among us, but that we may always give thanks for your healing power as we travel on the way to your kingdom. We ask this through Jesus Christ our Lord. Amen.

Sunday between October 16 and 22 inclusive

Preparation for Sunday
Daily: Psalm 119:97-104

Thursday
Jeremiah 26:1-15
Acts 17:22-34

Friday
Jeremiah 26:16-24
2 Timothy 2:14-26

Saturday
Jeremiah 31:15-26
Mark 10:46-52

Sunday
Jeremiah 31:27-34
Psalm 119:97-104
2 Timothy 3:14—4:5
Luke 18:1-8

Reflection on Sunday
Daily: Psalm 129

Monday
Jeremiah 38:14-28
1 Corinthians 6:1-11

Tuesday
Jeremiah 39:1-18
James 5:7-12

Wednesday
Jeremiah 50:1-7, 17-20
Luke 22:39-46

The General Rule of Discipleship
*To witness to Jesus Christ in the world and to follow his teachings
through acts of compassion, justice, worship, and devotion under the guidance of the Holy Spirit.*

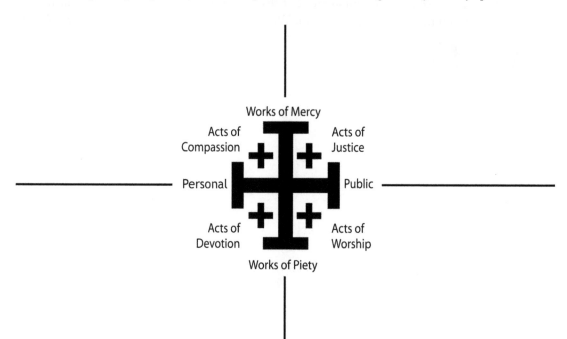

A Word from John Wesley

Hence we learn, that the first and great end of God's permitting the temptations which bring heaviness on his children, Is the trial of their faith, which is tried by these, even as gold by the fire. Now we know, gold tried in the fire is purified thereby; is separated from its dross. And so is faith in the fire of temptation; the more it is tried, the more it is purified;—yea, and not only purified, but also strengthened, confirmed, increased abundantly, by so many more proofs of the wisdom and power, the love and faithfulness, of God. This, then,—to increase our faith,—is one gracious end of God's permitting those manifold temptations.

Sermon 47: "Heaviness Through Manifold Temptations," § IV.2

A Hymn from Charles Wesley

The thing my God doth hate,
That I no more may do,
Thy creature, Lord, again create,
And all my soul renew;
My soul shall then, like thine,
Abhor the thing unclean,
And sanctified by love divine
Forever cease from sin.

That blessed law of thine,
Jesu, to me impart;
Thy Spirit's law of life divine,
O write it in my heart!
Implant it deep within,
Whence it may ne'er remove,
The law of liberty from sin,
The perfect law of love.

(*Collection*—1781, #339:1-2)

Prayers, Comments & Questions

O God, Spirit of righteousness, you temper judgment with mercy. Help us to live the covenant written upon our hearts so that when Christ returns, we may be found worthy to be received by grace into your presence. Amen.

Sunday between October 23 and 29 inclusive

Preparation for Sunday
Daily: Psalm 65

Thursday
Joel 1:1-20
2 Timothy 3:1-9

Friday
Joel 2:1-11
2 Timothy 3:10-15

Saturday
Joel 2:12-22
Luke 1:46b-55

Sunday
Joel 2:23-32
Psalm 65
2 Timothy 4:6-8, 16-18
Luke 18:9-14

Reflection on Sunday
Daily: Psalm 87

Monday
Joel 3:1-8
1 Peter 4:12-19

Tuesday
Joel 3:9-16
1 Peter 5:1-11

Wednesday
Joel 3:17-20
Matthew 21:28-32

The General Rule of Discipleship
To witness to Jesus Christ in the world and to follow his teachings
through acts of compassion, justice, worship, and devotion under the guidance of the Holy Spirit.

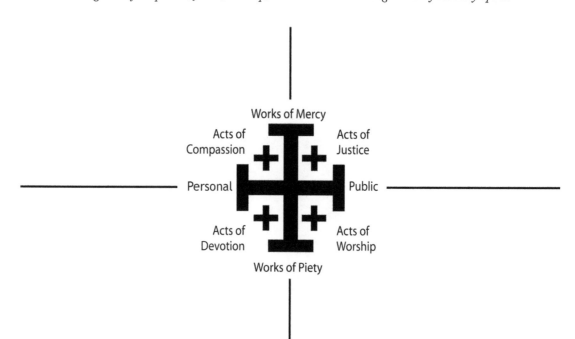

A Word from John Wesley

The denying ourselves and the taking up our cross, in the full extent of the expression, is not a thing of small concern: It is not expedient only, as are some of the circumstantials of religion; but it is absolutely, indispensably necessary, either to our becoming or continuing his disciples. . . . If we do not continually deny ourselves, we do not learn of Him, but of other masters. If we do not take up our cross daily, we do not come after Him, but after the world, or the prince of the world, or our own fleshly mind. If we are not walking in the way of the cross, we are not following Him; we are not treading in his steps; but going back from, or at least wide of, Him.

Sermon 48: "Self-Denial," ¶ 2

A Hymn from Charles Wesley

God of eternal truth and grace,
Thy faithful promise seal!
Thy word, thy oath to Abraham's race,
In us, even us, fulfill.

But is it possible that I
Should live, and sin no more?
Lord, if on thee I dare rely,
The faith shall bring the power.

On me that faith divine bestow
Which doth the mountain move;
And all my spotless life shall show
The omnipotence of love.

(*Collection—1781*, #341:1, 5-6)

Prayers, Comments & Questions

O Wellspring of salvation, we come to you in joy, for you have heard the prayers of the poor and raised up the lowly. Pour out your Spirit on young and old alike, that our dreams and visions may bring justice and peace to the world. Amen.

Sunday between October 30 and November 5 inclusive

Preparation for Sunday
Daily: Psalm 119:137-144

Thursday
Jeremiah 33:14-26
2 Corinthians 1:1-11

Friday
Habakkuk 1:5-17
2 Peter 1:1-11

Saturday
Habakkuk 2:5-11
John 8:39-47

Sunday
Habakkuk 1:1-4, 2:1-4
Psalm 119:137-144
2 Thessalonians 1:1-4, 11-12
Luke 19:1-10

Reflection on Sunday
Daily: Psalm 142

Monday
Habakkuk 2:12-20
1 Corinthians 5:9-13

Tuesday
Habakkuk 3:1-16
Jude 5-21

Wednesday
Habakkuk 3:17-19
Luke 19:11-27

The General Rule of Discipleship
To witness to Jesus Christ in the world and to follow his teachings
through acts of compassion, justice, worship, and devotion under the guidance of the Holy Spirit.

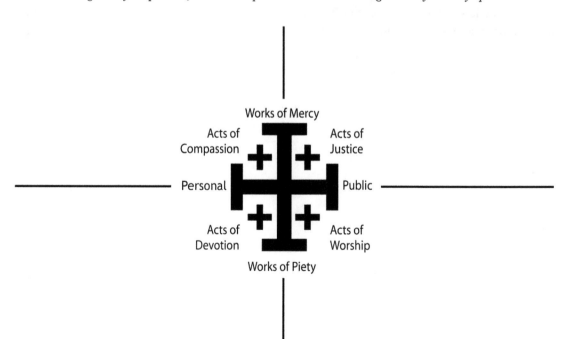

A Word from John Wesley

"Speak evil of no man," says the great Apostle:—As plain a command as, "Thou shalt do no murder." But who, even among Christians, regards this command? Yea, how few are there that so much as understand it? What is evil-speaking? It is not, as some suppose, the same with lying or slandering. All a man says may be as true as the Bible; and yet the saying of it is evil-speaking. For evil-speaking is neither more nor less than speaking evil of an absent person; relating something evil, which was really done or said by one that is not present when it is related. Suppose, having seen a man drunk, or heard him curse or swear, I tell this when he is absent; it is evil-speaking.

Sermon 49: "The Cure of Evil-Speaking," ¶ 1

A Hymn from Charles Wesley

O for a heart to praise my God,
A heart from sin set free;
A heart that always feels thy blood
So freely spilt for me!

A heart resigned, submissive, meek,
My great Redeemer's throne,
Where only Christ is heard to speak,
Where Jesus reigns alone.

O for a lowly, contrite heart,
Believing, true, and clean,
Which neither life nor death can part
From him that dwells within!

(*Collection*—1781, #342:1-3)

Prayers, Comments & Questions

In your Son you seek out and save the lost, O God, and invite us to the banquet of your eternal home. Visit your people with the joy of salvation, that we may rejoice in the riches of your forgiveness and reach out in welcome to share with others the feast of your love. Amen.

Sunday between November 6 and 12 inclusive

Preparation for Sunday
Daily: Psalm 145:1-5, 17-21

Thursday
Zechariah 1:1-17
Acts 22:22—23:11

Friday
Zechariah 6:9-15
Acts 24:10-23

Saturday
Haggai 1:1-15a
Luke 20:1-8

Sunday
Haggai 1:15b—2:9
Psalm 145:1-5, 17-21
or Psalm 98
2 Thess. 2:1-5, 13-17
Luke 20:27-38

Reflection on Sunday
Daily: Psalm 98

Monday
Haggai 2:10-19
2 Peter 1:16-21

Tuesday
Haggai 2:20-23
2 John 1-13

Wednesday
Zechariah 8:1-17
John 5:19-29

The General Rule of Discipleship
*To witness to Jesus Christ in the world and to follow his teachings
through acts of compassion, justice, worship, and devotion under the guidance of the Holy Spirit.*

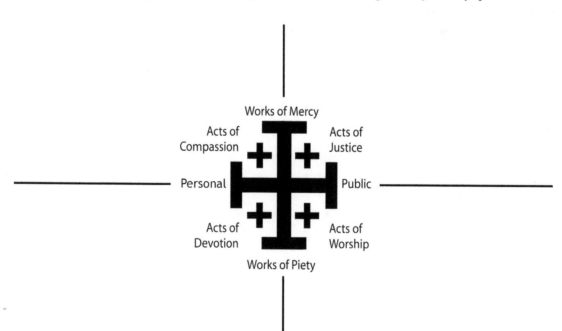

A Word from John Wesley

In order to see the ground and reason of this, consider, when the Possessor of heaven and earth brought you into being, and placed you in this world, he placed you here not as a proprietor, but a steward: As such he entrusted you, for a season, with goods of various kinds; but the sole property of these still rests in him, nor can be alienated from him. As you yourself are not your own, but his, such is, likewise, all that you enjoy. Such is your soul and your body, not your own, but God's. And so is your substance in particular. And he has told you, in the most clear and express terms, how you are to employ it for him, in such a manner, that it may be all an holy sacrifice, acceptable through Christ Jesus. And this light, easy service, he has promised to reward with an eternal weight of glory.

Sermon 50: "The Use of Money," § III.2

A Hymn from Charles Wesley

Ye happy sinners hear
The prisoner of the Lord,
And wait, till Christ appear
According to his word;
Rejoice in hope, rejoice with me,
We shall from all our sins be free.

The Lord our righteousness
We have long since received;
Salvation nearer is
Than when we first believed;
Rejoice in hope, rejoice with me,
We shall from all our sins be free.

(*Collection*—1781, #344:1-2)

Prayers, Comments & Questions

Almighty God, you hold all the powers of the universe within your hands, and we are your children. Turn us to the splendor of life in you, transforming us through Jesus Christ our Savior and strengthening us in every good deed and word. Amen.

Sunday between November 13 and 19 inclusive

Preparation for Sunday
Daily: Isaiah 12

Thursday
Isaiah 57:14-21
Romans 1:18-25

Friday
Isaiah 59:1-15a
2 Thessalonians 1:3-12

Saturday
Isaiah 59:15b-21
Luke 17:20-37

Sunday
Isaiah 65:17-25
Isaiah 12
2 Thessalonians 3:6-13
Luke 21:5-19

Reflection on Sunday
Daily: Psalm 76

Monday
Isaiah 60:17-22
Ephesians 4:25—5:2

Tuesday
Isaiah 66:1-13
1 Corinthians 10:23—11:1

Wednesday
Isaiah 66:14-24
Matthew 23:37—24:14

The General Rule of Discipleship
To witness to Jesus Christ in the world and to follow his teachings
through acts of compassion, justice, worship, and devotion under the guidance of the Holy Spirit.

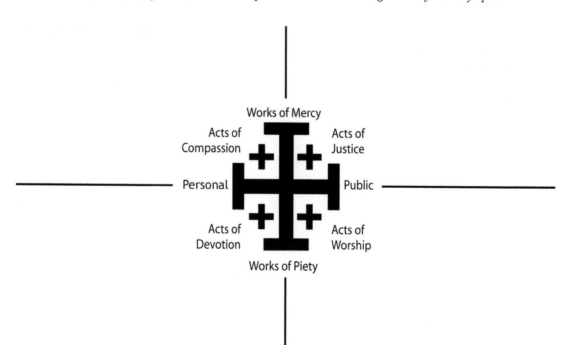

A Word from John Wesley

Thy Lord will farther inquire, "Hast thou been a wise and faithful steward with regard to the talents of a mixed nature which I lent thee? . . . Above all, wast thou a good steward of my grace, preventing, accompanying, and following thee? Didst thou duly observe, and carefully improve, all the influences of my Spirit . . . And when thou wast made a partaker of this Spirit, crying in thy heart, "Abba, Father," didst thou stand fast in the glorious liberty wherewith I made thee free? Didst thou from thenceforth present thy soul and body, all thy thoughts, thy words, and actions, in one flame of love, as a holy sacrifice, glorifying me with thy body and thy spirit? Then 'well done, good and faithful servant! Enter thou into the joy of thy Lord!'"

Sermon 51: "The Good Steward," § III.6

A Hymn from Charles Wesley

Jesu, my life, thyself apply,
Thy Holy Spirit breathe,
My vile affections crucify,
Conform me to thy death.

Conqu'ror of hell, and earth, and sin,
Still with thy rebel strive;
Enter my soul, and work within,
And kill and make alive!

More of thy life and more I have
As the old Adam dies;
Bury me, Saviour, in thy grave,
That I with thee may rise.

(*Collection*—1781, #346:1-3)

Prayers, Comments & Questions

O God, in Christ you give us hope for a new heaven and a new earth. Grant us wisdom to interpret the signs of our times, courage to stand in the time of trial, and faith to witness to your truth and love. Amen.

Reign of Christ *or* Christ the King

Preparation for Sunday
Daily: Luke 1:68-79

Thursday
Jeremiah 21:1-14
Hebrews 9:23-28

Friday
Jeremiah 22:1-17
1 Peter 1:3-9

Saturday
Jeremiah 22:18-30
Luke 18:15-17

Sunday
Jeremiah 23:1-6
Luke 1:68-79
Colossians 1:11-20
Luke 23:33-43

Reflection on Sunday
Daily: Psalm 117

Monday
Jeremiah 30:1-17
Revelation 21:5-27

Tuesday
Jeremiah 30:18-24
Revelation 22:8-21

Wednesday
Jeremiah 31:1-6
Luke 1:1-4

The General Rule of Discipleship
To witness to Jesus Christ in the world and to follow his teachings
through acts of compassion, justice, worship, and devotion under the guidance of the Holy Spirit.

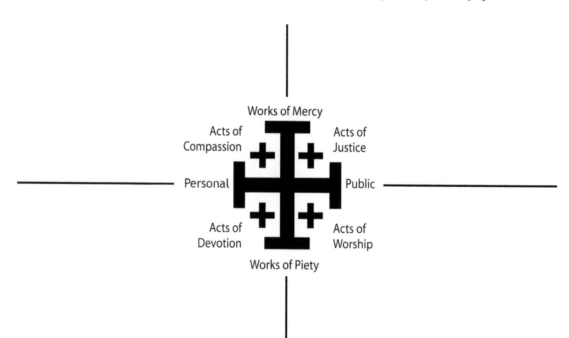

A Word from John Wesley

This is the original design of the Church of Christ. It is a body of men compacted together, in order, first, to save each his own soul; then to assist each other in working out their salvation; and, afterwards, as far as in them lies, to save all men from present and future misery, to overturn the kingdom of Satan, and set up the kingdom of Christ. And this ought to be the continued care and endeavour of every member of his Church; otherwise he is not worthy to be called a member thereof, as he is not a living member of Christ.

Sermon 52: "The Reformation of Manners," ¶ 2

A Hymn from Charles Wesley

Jesus, the conqu'ror reigns,
In glorious strength arrayed,
His kingdom over all maintains,
And bids the earth be glad.
Ye sons of men, rejoice
In Jesu's mighty love;
Lift up your heart, lift up your voice
To him who rules above.

Extol his kingly power,
Kiss the exalted Son
Who died, and lives to die no more
High on his Father's throne;
Our Advocate with God,
He undertakes our cause,
And spreads through all the earth abroad
The vict'ry of his cross.

(*Collection*—1781, #276,1-2)

Prayers, Comments & Questions

Shepherd of Israel, hear our prayer as your Son heard the plea of a criminal crucified with him. Gather into Christ's holy reign the broken, the sorrowing, and the sinner, that all may know wholeness, joy, and forgiveness. Amen.

Wesleyan Discipleship

Sermon 92: "On Zeal"

This sermon is an important word for Christians today. Wesley calls Christians to be zealous for Christ and his mission in the world. He helps us understand that true zeal is love, the love of God revealed in Christ crucified and risen. Followers of Jesus Christ are called by him to pursue holiness of heart and life, or universal love filling the heart and governing the life. — Steven W. Manskar

"It is good to be always zealously affected in a good thing."

Galatians 4:18

Rev. John Wesley
1781

1. There are few subjects in the whole compass of religion, that are of greater importance than this. For without zeal it is impossible, either to make any considerable progress in religion ourselves, or to do any considerable service to our neighbour, whether in temporal or spiritual things. And yet nothing has done more disservice to religion, or more mischief to mankind, than a sort of zeal which has for several ages prevailed, both in Pagan, Mahometan, and Christian nations. Insomuch that it may truly be said, pride, covetousness, ambition, revenge, have in all parts of the world slain their thousands; but zeal its ten thousands. Terrible instances of this have occurred in ancient times, in the most civilized heathen nations. To this chiefly were owing the inhuman persecutions of the primitive Christians; and, in later ages, the no less inhuman persecutions of the Protestants by the Church of Rome. It was zeal that kindled fires in our nation, during the reign of bloody Queen Mary. It was zeal that soon after made so many provinces of France a field of blood. It was zeal that murdered so many thousand unresisting Protestants, in the never-to-be-forgotten massacre of Paris. It was zeal that occasioned the still more horrid massacre in Ireland; the like whereof, both with regard to the number of the murdered, and the shocking circumstances wherewith many of those murders were perpetrated, I verily believe never occurred before since the world began. As to the other parts of Europe, an eminent German writer has taken immense pains to search both the records in various places and the most authentic histories, in order to gain some competent knowledge of the blood which has been shed since the Reformation, and computes that, partly by private persecution, partly by religious wars, in the course of forty years, reckoning from the year 1520, above forty millions of persons have been destroyed!

2. But is it not possible to distinguish right zeal from wrong? Undoubtedly it is possible. But it is difficult; such is the deceitfulness of the human heart; so skillfully do the passions justify themselves. And there are exceeding few treatises on the subject; at least in the English language. To this day I have seen or heard of only one sermon; and that was wrote above a hundred years ago, by Dr. Sprat, then Bishop of Rochester; so that it is now exceeding scarce.

3. I would gladly cast in my mite, by God's assistance, toward the clearing up this important question, in order to enable well meaning men, who are desirous of pleasing God, to distinguish true Christian zeal from its various counterfeits. And this is more necessary at this time than it has been for many years. Sixty years ago there seemed to be scarce any such thing as religious zeal left in the nation. People in general were wonderfully cool and undisturbed about that trifle, religion. But since then it is easy to observe, there has been a very considerable alteration. Many thousands, almost in every part of the nation, have felt a real desire to save their souls. And I am persuaded there is at this day more religious zeal in England, than there has been for a century past.

4. But has this zeal been of the right or the wrong kind? Probably both the one and the other. Let us see if we cannot separate these, that we may avoid the latter, and cleave to the former. In order to this, I would first inquire,

I. What is the nature of true Christian zeal?
II. What are the properties of it? And,
III. Draw some practical inferences.

I.

And, First, What is the nature of zeal in general, and of true Christian zeal in particular?

1. The original word, in its primary signification, means heat; such as the heat of boiling water. When it is figuratively applied to the mind, it means any warm emotion or affection. Sometimes it is taken for envy. So we render it, Acts 5:17, where we read, "The High Priest, and all that were with him, were filled with envy,"—*eplesthesan zelou* although it might as well be rendered, were filled with zeal. Sometimes, it is taken for anger and indignation; sometimes, for vehement desire. And when any of our passions are strongly moved on a religious account, whether for anything good, or against anything which we conceive to be evil, this we term, religious zeal.

2. But it is not all that is called religious zeal which is worthy of that name. It is not properly religious or Christian zeal, if it be not joined with charity. A fine writer (Bishop Sprat) carries the matter farther still. "It has been affirmed," says that great man, "no zeal is right, which is not charitable, but is mostly so. Charity or love, is not only one ingredient, but the chief ingredient in its composition." May we not go further still? May we not say, that true zeal is not mostly charitable, but wholly so?

That is, if we take charity, in St. Paul's sense, for love; the love of God and our neighbour. For it is a certain truth, (although little understood in the world,) that Christian zeal is all love. It is nothing else. The love of God and man fills up its whole nature.

3. Yet it is not every degree of that love, to which this appellation is given. There may be some love, a small degree of it, where there is no zeal. But it is, properly, love in a higher degree. It is fervent love. True Christian zeal is no other than the flame of love. This is the nature, the inmost essence, of it.

II.

1. From hence it follows, that the properties of love are the properties of zeal also. Now, one of the chief properties of love is humility: "Love is not puffed up." Accordingly, this is a property of true zeal: Humility is inseparable from it. As is the degree of zeal, such is the degree of humility: They must rise and fall together. The same love which fills a man with zeal for God, makes him little, and poor, and vile in his own eyes.

2. Another of the properties of love is meekness: Consequently, it is one of the properties of zeal. It teaches us to be meek, as well as lowly; to be equally superior to anger or pride. Like as the wax melts at the fire, so before this sacred flame all turbulent passions melt away, and leave the soul unruffled and serene.

3. Yet another property of love, and consequently of zeal, is unwearied patience: For "love endures all things." It arms the soul with entire resignation to all the disposals of Divine Providence, and teaches us to say, in every occurrence, "It is the Lord; let him do what seems him good." It enables us, in whatever station, therewith to be content; to repine at nothing, to murmur at nothing, "but in everything to give thanks."

4. There is a Fourth property of Christian zeal, which deserves to be more particularly considered. This we learn from the very words of the Apostle, "It is good to be zealously affected always" (not to have transient touches of zeal, but a steady, rooted disposition) "in a good thing:" In that which is good; for the proper object of zeal is, good in general; that is, everything that is good, really such, in the sight of God.

5. But what is good in the sight of God? What is that religion, wherewith God is always well pleased? How do the parts of this rise one above another, and what is the comparative value of them?

This is a point exceeding little considered, and therefore little understood. Positive divinity, many have some knowledge of. But few know anything of comparative divinity. I never saw but one tract upon this head; a sketch of which it may be of use to subjoin.

In a Christian believer love sits upon the throne which is erected in the inmost soul; namely, love of God and man, which fills the whole heart, and reigns without a rival. In a circle near the throne are all holy tempers;—longsuffering, gentleness, meekness, fidelity, temperance; and if any other were comprised in "the mind which was in Christ Jesus." In an exterior circle are all the works of mercy, whether to the souls or bodies of men. By these we exercise all holy tempers; by these we continually improve them, so that all these are real means of grace, although this is not commonly adverted to. Next to these are those that are usually termed works of piety;—reading and hearing the word, public, family, private prayer, receiving the Lord's Supper, fasting or abstinence. Lastly, that his followers may the more effectually provoke one another to love, holy tempers, and good works, our blessed Lord has united them together in one body, the Church, dispersed all over the earth; a little emblem of which, of the Church universal, we have in every particular Christian congregation.

6. This is that religion which our Lord has established upon earth, ever since the descent of the Holy Ghost on the day of Pentecost. This is the entire, connected system of Christianity: And thus the several parts of it rise one above another, from that lowest point, the assembling ourselves together, to the highest, love enthroned in the heart. And hence it is easy to learn the comparative value of every branch of religion. Hence also we learn a Fifth property of true zeal: That as it is always exercised *en kalo*, in that which is good, so it is always proportioned to that good, to the degree of goodness that is in its object.

7. For example. Every Christian ought, undoubtedly, to be zealous for the Church, bearing a strong affection to it, and earnestly desiring its prosperity and increase. He ought to be thus zealous, as for the Church universal, praying for it continually, so especially for that particular Church or Christian society whereof he himself is a member. For this; he ought to wrestle with God in prayer; meantime using every means in his power to enlarge its borders, and to strengthen his brethren, that they may adorn the doctrine of God our Saviour.

8. But he should be more zealous for the ordinances of Christ than for the Church itself; for prayer in public and private; for the Lord's Supper; for reading, hearing, and meditating on his word; and for the much-neglected duty of fasting. These he should earnestly recommend; first, by his example; and then by advice, by argument, persuasion, and exhortation, as often as occasion offers.

9. Thus should he show his zeal for works of piety; but much more for works of mercy; seeing "God will have mercy and not sacrifice;" that is, rather than sacrifice. Whenever, therefore, one interferes with the other, works of mercy are to be preferred. Even reading, hearing, prayer, are to be omitted, or to be postponed, "at charity's almighty call;" when we are called to relieve the distress of our neighbour, whether in body or soul.

10. But as zealous as we are for all good works, we should still he more zealous for holy tempers; for planting and promoting, both in our own souls, and in all we have any intercourse with, lowliness of

mind, meekness, gentleness, longsuffering, contentedness, resignation unto the will of God, deadness to the world and the things of the world, as the only means of being truly alive to God. For these proofs and fruits of living faith we cannot be too zealous. We should "talk of them as we sit in our house," and "when we walk by the way," and "when we lie down," and "when we rise up." We should make them continual matter of prayer; as being far more excellent than any outward works whatever: Seeing those will fail when the body drops off; but these will accompany us into eternity.

11. But our choicest zeal should be reserved for love itself, the end of the commandment, the fulfilling of the law. The Church, the ordinances, outward works of every kind, yea, all other holy tempers, are inferior to this, and rise in value only as they approach nearer and nearer to it. Here then is the great object of Christian zeal. Let every true believer in Christ apply, with all fervency of spirit, to the God and Father of our Lord Jesus Christ, that his heart may be more and more enlarged in love to God and to all mankind. This one thing let him do: Let him "press on to this prize of our high calling of God in Christ Jesus."

III.

It remains only to draw some practical inferences from the preceding observations.

1. And, First, if zeal, true Christian zeal, be nothing but the flame of love, then hatred, in every kind and degree, then every sort of bitterness toward them that oppose us, is so far from deserving the name of zeal, that it is directly opposite to it. If zeal be only fervent love, then it stands at the utmost distance from prejudice, jealousy, evil-surmising; seeing "love thinks no evil." Then bigotry of every sort, and, above all, the spirit of persecution, are totally inconsistent with it. Let not, therefore, any of these unholy tempers screen themselves under that sacred name. As all these are the works of the devil, let them appear in their own shape, and no longer under that specious disguise deceive the unwary children of God.

2. Secondly. If lowliness be a property of zeal, then pride is inconsistent with it. It is true, some degree of pride may remain after the love of God is shed abroad in the heart; as this is one of the last evils that is rooted out, when God creates all things new; but it cannot reign, nor retain any considerable power, where fervent love is found. Yea, were we to give way to it but a little, it would damp that holy fervour, and, if we did not immediately fly back to Christ, would utterly quench the Spirit.

3. Thirdly. If meekness be an inseparable property of zeal, what shall we say of those who call their anger by that name? Why, that they mistake the truth totally; that they, in the fullest sense, put darkness for light, and light for darkness. We cannot be too watchful against this delusion, because it spreads over the whole Christian world. Almost in all places, zeal and anger pass for equivalent terms; and exceeding few persons are convinced, that there is any difference between them. How commonly do we hear it said, "See how zealous the man is!" Nay, he cannot be zealous; that is

impossible, for he is in a passion; and passion is as inconsistent with zeal, as light with darkness, or heaven with hell!

It were well that this point were thoroughly understood. Let us consider it a little farther. We frequently observe one that bears the character of a religious man vehemently angry at his neighbour. Perhaps he calls his brother *Raca*, or Thou fool. He brings a railing accusation against him. You mildly admonish him of his warmth. He answers, "It is my zeal!" No: It is your sin, and, unless you repent of it, will sink you lower than the grave. There is much such zeal as this in the bottomless pit. Thence all zeal of this kind comes; and thither it will go, and you with it, unless you are saved from it before you go hence!

4. Fourthly. If patience, contentedness, and resignation, are the properties of zeal, then murmuring, fretfulness, discontent, impatience are wholly inconsistent with it. And yet how ignorant are mankind of this! How often do we see men fretting at the ungodly, or telling you they are out of patience with such or such things, and terming all this their zeal! O spare no pains to undeceive them! If it be possible, show them what zeal is; and convince them that all murmuring, or fretting at sin, is a species of sin, and has no resemblance of, or connexion with, the true zeal of the gospel.

5. Fifthly. If the object of zeal be that which is good, then fervour for any evil thing is not Christian zeal. I instance in idolatry, worshipping of angels, saints, images, the cross. Although, therefore, a man were so earnestly attached to any kind of idolatrous worship, that he would even "give his body to be burned," rather than refrain from it, call this bigotry or superstition, if you please, but call it not zeal; that is quite another thing.

From the same premises it follows, that fervour for indifferent things is not Christian zeal. But how exceedingly common is this mistake too! Indeed one would think that men of understanding could not be capable of such weakness. But, alas! the history of all ages proves the contrary. Who were men of stronger understandings than Bishop Ridley and Bishop Hooper? And how warmly did these, and other great men of that age, dispute about the sacerdotal vestments! How eager was the contention for almost a hundred years, for and against wearing a surplice! O shame to man! I would as soon have disputed about a straw or a barley-corn! And this, indeed, shall be called zeal! And why was it not rather called wisdom or holiness?

6. It follows also, from the same premises, that fervour for opinions is not Christian zeal. But how few are sensible of this! And how innumerable are the mischiefs which even this species of false zeal has occasioned in the Christian world! How many thousand lives have been cast away by those who were zealous for the Romish opinions! How many of the excellent ones of the earth have been cut off by zealots, for the senseless opinion of transubstantiation! But does not every unprejudiced person see, that this zeal is "earthly, sensual, devilish;" and that it stands at the utmost contrariety to that zeal which is here recommended by the Apostle?

What an excess of charity is it then which our great poet expresses, in his "Poem on the Last Day," where he talks of meeting in heaven—

Those who by mutual
    wounds expired,
By zeal for their distinct
    persuasions fired!

Zeal indeed! What manner of zeal was this, which led them to cut one another's throats? Those who were fired with this spirit, and died therein, will undoubtedly have their portion, not in heaven, (only love is there,) but in the "fire that never shall be quenched."

7. Lastly. If true zeal be always proportioned to the degree of goodness which is in its object, then should it rise higher and higher according to the scale mentioned above; according to the comparative value of the several parts of religion. For instance, all that truly fear God should be zealous for the Church; both for the catholic or universal Church, and for that part of it whereof they are members. This is not the appointment of men, but of God. He saw it was "not good for men to be alone," even in this sense, but that the whole body of his children should be "knit together, and strengthened, by that which every joint supplies." At the same time they should be more zealous for the ordinances of God; for public and private prayer, for hearing and reading the word of God, and for fasting, and the Lord's Supper. But they should be more zealous for works of mercy, than even for works of piety. Yet ought they to be more zealous still for all holy tempers, lowliness, meekness, resignation: But most zealous of all, for that which is the sum and the perfection of religion, the love of God and man.

8. It remains only to make a close and honest application of these things to our own souls. We all know the general truth, that "it is good to be always zealously affected in a good thing." Let us now, every one of us, apply it to his own soul in particular.

9. Those, indeed, who are still dead in trespasses and sins have neither part nor lot in this matter; nor those that live in any open sin, such as drunkenness, Sabbath-breaking, or profane swearing. These have nothing to do with zeal; they have no business at all even to take the word in their mouth. It is utter folly and impertinence for any to talk of zeal for God, while he is doing the works of the devil. But if you have renounced the devil and all his works, and have settled it in your heart, I will "worship the Lord my God, and him only will I serve," then beware of being neither cold nor hot; then be zealous for God. You may begin at the lowest step. Be zealous for the Church; more especially for that particular branch thereof wherein your lot is cast. Study the welfare of this, and carefully observe all the rules of it, for conscience' sake. But, in the mean time, take heed that you do not neglect any of the ordinances of God; for the sake of which, in a great measure, the Church itself was constituted: So that it would be highly absurd to talk of zeal for the Church, if you were not more

zealous for them. But are you more zealous for works of mercy, than even for works of piety? Do you follow the example of your Lord, and prefer mercy even before sacrifice? Do you use all diligence in feeding the hungry, clothing the naked, visiting them that are sick and in prison? And, above all, do you use every means in your power to save souls from death? If, as you have time, "you do good unto all men," though "especially to them that are of the household of faith," your zeal for the Church is pleasing to God: But if not, if you are not "careful to maintain good works," what have you to do with the Church? If you have not "compassion on your fellow-servants," neither will your Lord have pity on you. "Bring no more vain oblations." All your service is "an abomination to the Lord."

10. Are you better instructed than to put asunder what God has joined? Than to separate works of piety from works of mercy? Are you uniformly zealous of both? So far you walk acceptably to God; that is, if you continually bear in mind, that God "searches the heart and reins;" that "he is a Spirit, and they that worship him must worship him in spirit and in truth;" that, consequently, no outward works are acceptable to him, unless they spring from holy tempers, without which no man can have a place in the kingdom of Christ and God.

11. But of all holy tempers, and above all others, see that you be most zealous for love. Count all things loss in comparison of this, the love of God and all mankind. It is most sure, that if you give all your goods to feed the poor, yea, and your body to be burned, and have not humble, gentle, patient love, it profits you nothing. O let this be deep engraven upon your heart: "All is nothing without love!"

12. Take then the whole of religion together, just as God has revealed it in his word; and be uniformly zealous for every part of it, according to its degree of excellence, grounding all your zeal on the one foundation, "Jesus Christ and him crucified;" holding fast this one principle, "The life I now live, I live by faith in the Son of God, who loved ME, and gave himself for ME." Proportion your zeal to the value of its object. Be calmly zealous, therefore, First, for the Church; "the whole state of Christ's Church militant here on earth;" and in particular for that branch thereof with which you are more immediately connected. Be more zealous for all those ordinances which our blessed Lord hath appointed, to continue therein to the end of the world. Be more zealous for those works of mercy, those "sacrifices wherewith God is well pleased," those marks whereby the Shepherd of Israel will know his sheep at the last day. Be more zealous still for holy tempers, for longsuffering, gentleness, meekness, lowliness, and resignation: But be most zealous of all for love, the queen of all graces, the highest perfection in earth or heaven, the very image of the invisible God, as in men below, so in angels above. For "God is love; and he that dwells in love, dwells in God, and God in him."

The Nature, Design, and General Rules of Our United Societies

In the latter end of the year 1739 eight or ten persons came to Mr. Wesley, in London, who appeared to be deeply convinced of sin, and earnestly groaning for redemption. They desired, as did two or three more the next day, that he would spend some time with them in prayer, and advise them how to flee from the wrath to come, which they saw continually hanging over their heads. That he might have more time for this great work, he appointed a day when they might all come together, which from thenceforward they did every week, namely, on Thursday in the evening. To these, and as many more as desired to join with them (for their number increased daily), he gave those advices from time to time which he judged most needful for them, and they always concluded their meeting with prayer suited to their several necessities.

This was the rise of the **United Society**, first in Europe, and then in America. Such a society is no other than "a company of men having the *form* and seeking the *power* of godliness, united in order to pray together, to receive the word of exhortation, and to watch over one another in love, that they may help each other to work out their salvation."

That it may the more easily be discerned whether they are indeed working out their own salvation, each society is divided into smaller companies, called **classes**, according to their respective places of abode. There are about twelve persons in a class, one of whom is styled the **leader**. It is his duty:

1. To see each person in his class once a week at least, in order:
   - to inquire how their souls prosper;
   - to advise, reprove, comfort or exhort, as occasion may require;
   - to receive what they are willing to give toward the relief of the preachers, church, and poor.

2. To meet the ministers and the stewards of the society once a week, in order:
   - to inform the minister of any that are sick, or of any that walk disorderly and will not be reproved;
   - to pay the stewards what they have received of their several classes in the week preceding.

There is only one condition previously required of those who desire admission into these societies: "a desire to flee from the wrath to come, and to be saved from their sins." But wherever this is really fixed in the soul it will be shown by its fruits.

It is therefore expected of all who continue therein that they should continue to evidence their desire of salvation,

First: By doing no harm, by avoiding evil of every kind, especially that which is most generally practiced, such as:

- The taking of the name of God in vain.
- The profaning the day of the Lord, either by doing ordinary work therein or by buying or selling.
- Drunkenness: buying or selling spirituous liquors, or drinking them, unless in cases of extreme necessity.
- Slaveholding; buying or selling slaves.
- Fighting, quarreling, brawling, brother going to law with brother; returning evil for evil, or railing for railing; the using many words in buying or selling.
- The buying or selling goods that have not paid the duty.
- The giving or taking things on usury—i.e., unlawful interest.
- Uncharitable or unprofitable conversation; particularly speaking evil of magistrates or of ministers.
- Doing to others as we would not they should do unto us.
- Doing what we know is not for the glory of God, as:
  » The putting on of gold and costly apparel.
  » The taking such diversions as cannot be used in the name of the Lord Jesus.
  » The singing those songs, or reading those books, which do not tend to the knowledge or love of God.
  » Softness and needless self-indulgence.
  » Laying up treasure upon earth.
  » Borrowing without a probability of paying; or taking up goods without a probability of paying for them.

It is expected of all who continue in these societies that they should continue to evidence their desire of salvation,

Secondly: By doing good; by being in every kind merciful after their power; as they have opportunity, doing good of every possible sort, and, as far as possible, to all men:

To their bodies, of the ability which God giveth, by giving food to the hungry, by clothing the naked, by visiting or helping them that are sick or in prison.

To their souls, by instructing, reproving, or exhorting all we have any intercourse with; trampling under foot that enthusiastic doctrine that "we are not to do good unless our hearts be free to it."

By doing good, especially to them that are of the household of faith or groaning so to be; employing them preferably to others; buying one of another, helping each other in business, and so much the more because the world will love its own and them only.

By all possible diligence and frugality, that the gospel be not blamed.

By running with patience the race which is set before them, denying themselves, and taking up their cross daily; submitting to bear the reproach of Christ, to be as the filth and offscouring of the world; and looking that men should say all manner of evil of them falsely, for the Lord's sake.

It is expected of all who desire to continue in these societies that they should continue to evidence their desire of salvation,

Thirdly: By attending upon all the ordinances of God; such are:

- The public worship of God.
- The ministry of the Word, either read or expounded.
- The Supper of the Lord.
- Family and private prayer.
- Searching the Scriptures.
- Fasting or abstinence.

These are the General Rules of our societies; all of which we are taught of God to observe, even in his written Word, which is the only rule, and the sufficient rule, both of our faith and practice. And all these we know his Spirit writes on truly awakened hearts. If there be any among us who observe them not, who habitually break any of them, let it be known unto them who watch over that soul as they who must give an account. We will admonish him of the error of his ways. We will bear with him for a season. But then, if he repent not, he hath no more place among us. We have delivered our own souls.

From *The Book of Discipline of The United Methodist Church—2016*, ¶ 104.

The General Rule of Discipleship

The General Rule of Discipleship is a contemporary re-statement of the General Rules. It distills the General Rules down to a single, straightforward statement that can be easily memorized:

**To witness to Jesus Christ in the world and
to follow his teachings through acts of
compassion, justice, worship, and devotion
under the guidance of the Holy Spirit.**

The General Rule of Discipleship is a succinct description of discipleship. It begins by acknowledging that a disciple is one who is a witness to Jesus Christ. This tells us that he or she knows Jesus and can tell others who he is and what he is doing in the world.

A disciple lives and witnesses to Jesus Christ in the world. This acknowledges that discipleship is not primarily about the enjoyment of personal blessings. It is much more about joining Christ and his mission in the world. When Christ calls us to follow him, he calls us to follow him into the world he loves.

A disciple follows Jesus by obeying his teachings. The General Rule tells us that discipleship is a relationship with Christ. Disciples participate in practices that draw them to Christ and keep them with him. Jesus said in Luke 9:23:

> "If any want to become my followers, let them deny themselves and take
> up their cross daily and follow me."

Self-denial is loving the way Jesus loves. In the context of discipleship, grace enables you to love as God loves.

The cross disciples must take up each day is obedience to Jesus' teaching summarized in Matthew 22:37-40:

> "You shall love the Lord your God with all your heart, and with all your
> soul, and with all your mind." This is the greatest and first commandment.
> And a second is like it: "You shall love your neighbor as yourself." On these
> two commandments hang all the law and the prophets.

Disciples practice loving God (the cross' vertical axis) through acts of worship and devotion. They respond to God's love by loving those whom God loves, as God loves them through acts of compassion and justice (the cross' horizontal axis). As disciples take up the cross of obedience to Jesus' commands, they open themselves to grace and grow in holiness of heart and life.

Finally, the General Rule of Discipleship tells us that those witnessing to Jesus Christ in the world and following his teachings are guided by the Holy Spirit. This tells us that disciples cannot follow Jesus alone, by their own strength. Only the Holy Spirit, working in them by grace, makes discipleship and subsequent growth in holiness of heart and life possible.

The General Rule of Discipleship helps disciples to maintain balance between all the teachings of Jesus. This balance is represented by the Jerusalem cross (below). The support and accountability provided by a Covenant Discipleship group helps disciples to walk with Christ in the world by practicing both works of mercy (loving the neighbor) and works of piety (loving God). It also helps to maintain balance between the personal and public dimensions of discipleship.

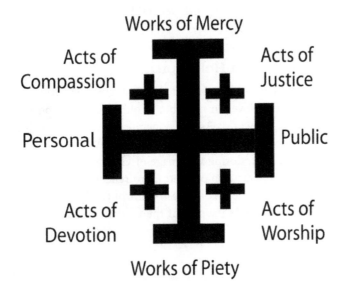

Works of Mercy

Jesus teaches his followers to live their professed love for God through loving whom God loves. *Acts of compassion* are acts of kindness, doing good, that help another person. Jesus teaches his followers to not only help others, but to also ask why people are hungry, homeless, refugees, and so on. He calls Christians to work together with other people of faith to be advocates to institutions and systems to work for the common good in *acts of justice*. They are how Christians work together to do no harm by avoiding and opposing evil.

Works of Piety

Christians participate in their relationship with God through *acts of worship* and *acts of devotion*. John Wesley names three acts of worship in the third General Rule: the public worship of God; the ministry of the word, either read or expounded; and the Lord's Supper. The assembly of the congregation give themselves in service to the Triune God through these social practices of praise and thanksgiving. Christians nurture their personal relationship with God in *acts of devotion*. Wesley names three essential acts of devotion in the third General Rule: private and family prayer; searching the Scriptures; and fasting or abstinence.

. . . under the guidance of the Holy Spirit

The Holy Spirit is Christ's presence working in us to remind us of his commands to love God with all our heart, soul, and mind, and to love our neighbor as ourselves. The Spirit supplies the grace we need to obey and follow Jesus in the world. As we cooperate with that grace, it flows through us for others and for the world. We become a channel of God's love. As love flows through us, the Holy Spirit heals our sin-damaged heart, restoring the image of God to wholeness. New heart habits, or holy tempers, are formed as our character more and more reflects Jesus: love, joy, peace, patience, kindness, generosity, faithfulness, gentleness, and self-control (Gal. 5:22-23). This is what Wesley calls "holiness of heart and life," which is the goal of the Christian life.

Holy Habits

Small groups provide the support and accountability we all need to form holy habits of compassion, justice, worship, and devotion. These habits move us to grow and mature in holiness of heart and life. John Wesley succinctly describes how Christians are formed:

"In a Christian believer love sits upon the throne which is erected in the inmost soul; namely, love of God and man, which fills the whole heart, and reigns without a rival. In a circle near the throne are all holy tempers: longsuffering, gentleness, meekness, fidelity, temperance; and if any other were comprised in 'the mind which was in Christ Jesus.' In an exterior circle are all the works of mercy, whether to the souls or bodies of men. By these we exercise all holy tempers; by these we continually improve them, so that all these are real means of grace, although this is not commonly adverted to.

Next to these are those that are usually termed works of piety: reading and hearing the word, public, family, private prayer, receiving the Lord's Supper, fasting or abstinence. Lastly, that his followers may the more effectually provoke one another to love, holy tempers, and good works, our blessed Lord has united them together in one body, the Church, dispersed all over the earth; a little emblem of which, of the Church universal, we have in every particular Christian congregation."

John Wesley, Sermon 92: "On Zeal", § II.5

Covenant Discipleship Groups

Covenant

. . . is God's word for "relationship." Covenant is God's way of **love**. Covenant tells us that God seeks and keeps relationships with others. The nature of God's covenant is self-giving love. Jesus Christ is God's covenant love in flesh and blood. We experience this love as **grace**; responsible grace. It is God's hand, open and outstretched to the world.

Christians are people who accept God's offer of covenant love in the water of baptism. They respond by turning away from sin and accepting the freedom and power God gives to resist evil. They confess Jesus Christ as Savior, put all their trust in his grace, and promise to serve him as Lord within the community of the church. Christians understand that the life of covenant love cannot be lived alone; it requires a community of prayer, forgiveness, and love.

Christians are covenant people.

Discipleship

. . . is how Christians live out their covenant with God. It is the way of life shaped by the teachings of Jesus Christ, summarized by him in Mark 12:30-31:

> "You shall love the Lord your God with all your heart, and with all your
> soul, and with all your mind, and with all your strength. . . . you shall
> love you neighbor as yourself."

A *disciple* is a person striving to conform his or her life to the life of a beloved teacher. A disciple seeks to become *like* the teacher. Disciples of Jesus Christ are Christians who align their own desires, goals, and habits with the desires, goals, and habits of Jesus Christ.

The apostle Paul describes the goal of discipleship in Philippians 2:5: "Let the same mind be in you that was in Christ Jesus."

Groups

. . . are discipleship incubators. It takes a community of love and forgiveness to make disciples.

Jesus gave his disciples a new commandment:

> ". . . love one another. Just as I have loved you, you also should love one another. By this everyone will know that you are my disciples, if you have love for one another" (John 13:34-35).

Disciples obey this new commandment when they meet regularly in small groups. They pray for one another, the church, and the world. They also give an account of how they have walked with Jesus in the world since they last met. The group works together to help one another become more dependable and mature disciples of Jesus Christ and leaders in discipleship for the church's mission in the world.

Wesleyan Disciple-making

Small groups that focus on mutual accountability and support for discipleship are the "method" of Methodism. These groups have their roots firmly planted in the Wesleyan tradition. The roots go even deeper when you consider that John Wesley described Methodism as his attempt to re-tradition "primitive" Christianity. He said:

> "a Methodist is one who has 'the love of God shed abroad in his heart by the Holy Ghost given unto him (or her)'"–from "The Character of a Methodist"

Covenant Discipleship groups are a way of helping Christians to grow in loving God with all their heart, soul, mind, and strength and love their neighbor as themselves. They are a proven and effective way of forming **leaders in discipleship** who in turn disciple others and help the congregation to live out its mission with Christ in the world.

Covenant Discipleship groups form Christ-centered people who lead Christ-centered congregations that participate in Christ's ongoing work of preparing the world for the coming reign of God, on earth as it is in heaven (Matthew 6:10; Luke 11:2).

The General Rule of Discipleship

. . . helps Covenant Discipleship group members to practice a balanced and varied discipleship. The General Rule is a contemporary re-statement of The General Rules John Wesley developed for the Methodist societies in 1742. It is simple and elegant:

> **"To witness to Jesus Christ in the world and to follow his teachings through acts of compassion, justice, worship, and devotion under the guidance of the Holy Spirit."**

Covenant Discipleship groups write a covenant that spells out how they will follow the teachings of Jesus Christ in their daily lives, shaped by the General Rule. The group's covenant serves as the agenda for the weekly one-hour meeting.

Covenant Discipleship Groups Are . . .

- up to seven people who meet for one hour each week
- guided by a covenant they write, shaped by the General Rule of Discipleship
- where Christians give a weekly account of how they have witnessed to Jesus Christ in the world and followed his teachings, guided by the group's covenant.
- where Christians help one another become more dependable disciples of Jesus Christ.
- a proven and effective way of nurturing and identifying leaders in discipleship the church needs to live out its mission with Christ in the world.

To Learn More . . .

visit the website at http://umcdiscipleship.org/covenantdiscipleship

Contact: Director of Adult Discipleship
PO Box 340003
Nashville, TN 37203-0003
Email: cdgroups@umcdiscipleship.org
Telephone: (877) 899-2780 (toll free)

Recommended Resources

Accountable Discipleship: Living in God's Household by Steven W. Manskar (Discipleship Resources, 2003)

    Provides biblical, theological and historic foundations for Covenant Discipleship.

Disciples Making Disciples: Guide for Covenant Discipleship Groups and Class Leaders by Steven W. Manskar (Discipleship Resources, 2016)

    Essential resource for congregational leaders and Covenant Discipleship group members. Provides valuable information on how to form groups, how to write a covenant, and how to lead a meeting.

Everyday Disciples: Covenant Discipleship with Youth by Chris Wilterdink (Discipleship Resources, 2016)

    This book is for pastors and youth workers. It provides ideas for youth ministry that effectively help middle school, senior high, and college students grow in holiness of heart and life.

Family the Forming Center: A Vision of the Role of Family in Spiritual Formation by Marjorie J. Thompson (Upper Room Books, 1998)

    Thompson's book provides a theological framework that enhances understanding of family.

Forming Christian Disciples: The Role of Covenant Discipleship and Class Leaders in the Congregation by David Lowes Watson (Wipf & Stock, 2002)

    This is an essential resource for pastors. Watson provides the historic, biblical, and theological rationale for Covenant Discipleship groups and Class Leaders. He helps the pastors understand their role in the congregation's disciple-making mission.

Growing Everyday Disciples: Covenant Discipleship with Children by Melanie Gordon, Susan Groseclose, and Gayle Quay (Discipleship Resources, 2016)

    This book is a resource for pastors and leaders responsible for the Christian formation of elementary school age children. It is excellent preparation for confirmation.

Help us to help each other, Lord,
Each other's cross to bear;
Let all their friendly aid afford,
And feel each other's care.

Touched by the lodestone of thy love,
Let all our hearts agree,
And ever toward each other move,
And ever move toward thee.

CHARLES WESLEY

Put your Covenant Discipleship group covenant here.

Notes

Notes

Notes

Notes

Notes

CPSIA information can be obtained
at www.ICGtesting.com
Printed in the USA
BVHW090928080921
616260BV00013B/237